ALCHEMY

ALCHEMY

THE AUTOBIOGRAPHY OF
THE ANGEL OF BENGAL

by

RYTASHA

EBURY PRESS
LONDON

First Published in 1992 by Ebury Press
an imprint of the Random Century Group
20 Vauxhall Bridge Road
London SW1V 2SA

A catalogue record for this book is available
from the British Library.

ISBN 0-09177-064-5

Typeset in Linotronic Times by
SX Composing Ltd, Rayleigh, Essex

Printed and bound by
Mackays of Chatham Ltd, Chatham, Kent

CHAPTER 1

It was the night of iron ore, salt, sulphur and snow that brought the Angel of Death to the city. He had come with the blizzard, which had waited patiently by the Staten Island Ferry before slicing through the massive canyons of Wall Street and up the East Side leaving the avenues lacquer-like ice, then over the bridges glittering on the throats of the black rivers, till it swirled into Central Park, danced among the ice-enamelled trees, buried the bushes in plump crystal drifts and turned the starry-sky night opaque-white over New York City on December 22, 1948 at 11 pm.

As the Angel soared over the city, he chanted the names of God into the snowstormy night. His face was as white as melted light, his eyes sapphires set in compassion, and his hair black with the knowledge of unknowing. Around his neck he wore a garland of skulls and his feet were as bare as humility.

From the sky he could see many parties for it was just

before Christmas. In the powder room of the Waldorf Astoria a beautiful woman in white satin and fabulous jewels applied another coat of 'Fire and Ice' to her lips before going back into a charity ball; down in Greenwich Village a group of young people were delighted with the snow and called and laughed and threw snowballs and were told to shut up for their troubles before a window was slammed down with a righteous harrumph.

In Harlem the Angel watched a small boy carefully cut a star out of an old newspaper to hang at the top of a pine branch he had found in an alley. While on Mott Street in Little Italy an old woman sat and studied a picture of a fresh-faced boy in uniform who would never come home for Christmas, and six Santa Clauses rode the No. 20 bus back down to the Bowery. Oh! and Father O'Malley falling asleep at his prayers.

As he flew his wing cast a shadow and people in warm rooms who a moment ago had been laughing suddenly felt melancholy. While a wise man living on the Lower East Side looked up and saluted, a drunk in a doorway off 42nd Street cursed and gulped more Thunderbird and a woman in Horn & Hardarts eating a slice of coconut-cream pie put down her fork.

At 59th and Central Park South, as he passed over my bedroom, his wing tore at the edge of sleep, its shadowy hulk pressing down on my chest with such force that I felt that I was suffocating. Alone in the empty apartment I struggled desperately with all the small strength of my six years against my nightmare fear of death.

I could see my toy box across the room and Thumper the rabbit where he had fallen out of bed. Holding tightly to Sailor Boy I inched the dial of the radio millimetre by millimetre into the ether looking for a story to distract me. If only I could find Superman or the Lone Ranger then sleep might steal up and whisk me to normal morning with my clothes laid out on a chair and Daddy would put a drop of his coffee in my milk; but tonight there is only music and that doesn't work. Wretched, I pick up the phone.

It doesn't take long for my father to arrive. He comes straight away from a dinner at the St Moritz, stars of snow melting on his shoulders, the cold still on his coat.

'Daddy, I don't feel well,' I say, as he puts a concerned hand on my forehead. Finding it cool, he tenderly brushes back the hair from my face and in his best bedside manner asks if I have pain. 'No.' 'Are you nauseous?' 'No.' 'Does it hurt here? . . . here?' 'No.'

He tucks Thumper and Sailor Boy into Grandma's blue afghan, admonishing them, 'Now you boys behave yourselves,' and sitting on the edge of the bed, his kind face grave, he tells us the story of *The Boy Who Cried Wolf*.

Curled up under the covers, warm as toast, the snow falling heavily outside the window I hold his hand spicy with aftershave to my cheek, inhaling the luxurious aroma of rosy wellbeing and listen, drowsily hypnotized, as the story unfolds. Safe now, I float dreaming out into the silent night, slowly rise up and over the city through layers of snow and stars and head gently towards morning.

*   *   *   *

On hot summer nights I bathe my forehead in the cool green air of the lilac tree outside my bedroom window and study assiduously a crack that has drawn a landscape on the wall – looking for visions, or perhaps a sheep.

My mother comes to kiss me goodnight on her way to a ball. She leans over my bed dressed in yards of tulle shimmering with paillettes. Like a little bird in my white nest I lift my face again and again for kisses. 'One more, one more,' I beg, my arms around her neck. 'Enough,' she laughs, extricating herself, leaving only the scent of her perfume, a blend of patchouli, rose, neroli and musk – her tender distillation. 'Right to sleep my darling, no reading now,' she says. I gaze adoringly at her, my hand on my book under the sheet.

When it is safe I take out my book with the picture of Joan of Arc on the cover. The Maid of Orleans – armoured habit – schismatic haircut. How I envy her conversations with the angels. On Sterling Road I chew my lip and look at the ceiling to see if someone might have something to say to me. Never mind that I'm afraid of horses; tonight I thunder over the fields of France with my soldiers, carrying the banner of the Holy Trinity, Jesus Maria, and the Burgundian betrayal – and the king's (first lesson). High in the tower she faces her inquisitors. Her purity condemns her to the green oak which gives the fiercest heat, the flames licking up everything but her heart. I weep luxuriant tears enjoying my martyrdom.

Suddenly my faith trembles. Frightened I throw myself on the floor. 'Oh dear God – not fire,' I pray.

On my mother's side I am descended from knights of the Teutonic order, the Carolingians, the Ottonian Systems, and the Saxons, that blue race who, cold-lipped, conquered Baltic coasts; merchant princes of the Hanseatic Leagues who married money. Minor aristocrats of 'blood and iron'.

And on my father's side, barbarians probably, or worse. Fanatical scholars who lay down under foul-smelling furs and rose up with sons to die of czars and pogroms carrying their dark bloodline in the Law and the Ark of the Covenant across Mother Russia.

My mother is my world. I adore her. As a child she had seen an angel, but where an angel might lead she chose not to follow. She chose life instead. She grounded herself in it. She was busy with it in all its practical detail from morning till night.

She is beautiful, though not a beauty – she has too much personality. Hers is the healthy darkness of swimming-pool suntans, a darkness without mystery. If there are mysteries, they are concealed as she conceals her lips, painting on a movie-star mouth with its slangy American smile.

She loves jewels and always wears the huge round diamond and thick gold band of marriage together with a heavy pink gold bracelet whose raspberries of rubies conceal a watch she never winds. Her hands, which she uses as an accessory are elegant, but fully capable of opening a jar. Mother gets what she wants. She is voluptuous, fleshful and rich; and always on a diet.

In the mornings I cuddle in her lap as she talks on the phone, organizing cocktails and dinner, cajoling the plumber, consulting the butcher. My head on her soft bosom I half listen to the buzzing of words as though they are a foreign language, soothing as a lullaby. 'Times a fleeting,' she says and off she goes full of plans for a day of shopping, luncheon at Schraft's and later, if I'm good, tea at the Plaza.

The Plaza Hotel floats majestically on New York afternoons. Tea is served in the Palm Court accompanied by violinists who give me the giggles and where 'Mademoiselle' can always have two choices from the exquisite French pastries. With great ceremony the two-tiered cart is wheeled to our table. I look carefully at the square yellow cakes with sugary pink frosting, the flaky, crusted tarts, their geometrically sliced apples encased in a golden honey varnish, the hot-house strawberries, their studded skins waiting to be sluiced with double cream; there are great slabs of Black Forest cake adorned with maraschino cherries, tart lemon meringue pie, and always a cut glass bowl of stewed fruits, figs and prunes in a thick sweet syrup. After long and concentrated deliberation I invariably choose what I always choose; a chocolate eclair and a Napoleon. My mother, ever mindful of calories, has the lemon meringue pie. 'It's all air,' she says as she lifts a forkful to her mouth.

All around ladies in stylish suits with tiny hats perched on their heads bend toward each other in animated conversation, their hushed voices barely audible over the clink of heavy silver, the tinkling of water on to ice cubes in frosted crystal.

Mother, tired from shopping, wearing a large cartwheel hat of black straw sits surrounded by boxes with the smart labels of the Lilliputian Bazaar at Best and Co., Bergdorf Goodman, and Saks Fifth Avenue.

My father can never understand the intricacies, the subtle exultation of shopping. The search for an ideal. The dress that would make you into a beauty, the lipstick that practically guarantees kisses, the boots that have an adventure built in. 'No,' he says somewhat wryly, 'their mariage is the perfect arrangement, an equal partnership.' He makes the money and she spends it.

My mother chain-smokes the monogrammed cigarettes my father orders for her at Sherman's and talks about life: the importance of money, of breeding and beauty, that men are hunters and one must never surrender everything to them, what colours suit the complexion, jewellery, which wine glass, which the fish fork, the efficacy of white collars, beauty sleep, and the getting and holding of men, all of which she's expert in. I participate in this womanly ritual passed down from mother to daughter, this conspiracy to hold to the earth, to succeed at security.

She was born in Hamburg on 2 November 1902, daughter of a notorious baron whose family had owned most of the marzipan factories in Germany. The baron, finding himself in difficulty in the stock market crash of '29 took the best suite at the Waldorf Astoria, ordered champagne, and dressing formally for the occasion, killed himself! My mother had lived most of her life in America. Growing up in a large brownstone on Riverside Drive and later attending Southern Seminary in Buena Vista, Virginia. My grandfather had emigrated because his family did not approve of the beautiful Titian-haired singer he had fallen passionately in love with and married. It was a love match the family could not countenance. They turned their back. They declared him dead.

By the time mother met my father, she had been married twice. Her first husband Tommy Paley, whose family founded CBS, was an attorney who spent most of his time playing polo. Her second, Al Staehle was an artist who together with Al Dorn started 'The Famous Artist School'. He designed the *Saturday Evening Post* covers and created one of the most popular characters in American illustrating; the naughty cocker spaniel Butch.

She was divorced and on her own having been successfully a fashion designer, headed her own advertising agency, and become editor-in-chief of *Miss America* magazine. Now she was handling the advertising for Helena Rubenstein.

In the middle of the night the phone would ring. 'Thea? You are awake?' Madame would ask. 'I have an idea for the advertising campaign. We need to discuss.' Mother would slip her full-length white mink over her nightgown and jump into a taxi to travel the short distance to 265 Park Avenue. The large apartment was a museum. Madame was having the first of several portraits painted by Salvador Dali. When Dali first met mother he invited her to his studio at the St Regis, but she never found the time to go. Madame would be waiting in an oriental robe looking like a cross between a Polish peasant, which she was, and the last empress of China, which she wasn't; her black hair pulled back so severely into a bun it scalped her face, her pudgy fingers loaded with the gaudy rings she collected. Madame kept cardboard cartons of jewellery in her closet and liked nothing better than unfastening an expensive brooch or sliding a ring from her finger and giving it to some amazed and forever grateful reporter or buyer.

The idea for the advertising campaign would turn out to be nothing more than a case of insomnia. The ladies would retire to the dining room where they would proceed to play away the night in endless games of gin rummy and cups of tea.

When she met my father, he was a young doctor who had only his brilliance to recommend him. He was from a Russian immigrant family, so poor he had only been able to go to university because his brother, the eldest son, had come home from school early one wintry afternoon and gone to bed sick. By the morning he was dead. So my father inherited his brother's estate and became the sole beneficiary of the dream.

It was while he was a resident in neurosurgery at Doctor's Hospital that he met and fell in love with my mother. She couldn't stand him, and in the way of such things married him ten days later. She always maintained that she didn't love him when she married him, but that she was 'sick of being alone, sick of going out with men who took you to dinner and later tried to squeeze it out of you,' and because at thirty-nine she deeply wanted a baby. A year after they were married she fell in love with him.

And nine months later I am born into the Second World War, which had taken my father, now a major in the army, all over the country setting up neurosurgical centres to treat the wounded.

My godfather is Prince Michael Evlanoff, a former member of the Czar's Imperial Court and married to Elizabeth Arden. 'Please call me Michael,' he says, 'This iss Americka.' Helena Rubenstein comes to the hospital with a beautiful christening dress for me and to ask how soon mother will be returning to work.

My first eight years we lived in New York City at the Essex House, a stately granite palace which flies flags of blue and white, red, stars and stripes above a lobby hung with chandeliers that give a muted glow to the rich rococo and marble interior. Among the bustle of elegant people below, women with furs thrown back casually over suits wait while their men who control out-of-state empires, big-deal men, full of blood money and pomade check them into suites. Young bellboys dressed to look like monkeys with pillbox hats fastened under their chins, carry messages on silver salvers, and yes ma'am and no sir, up and down the red runners, past mountains of monogrammed luggage.

I am eating lunch in lonely splendour in the Wedgwood blue dining room sitting on two telephone books, playing with the peas in the Chicken à la King my mother has rung down and ordered for me. I gaze out of the window across to Central Park soundless behind the cold glass, see children going to play chaperoned by governesses; their mouths open to make the round O of laughter.

The Essex House has an old-world elegance and only lets the side down once that I know of, when the electricity fails in the first two letters of the large sign atop the building and 'THE SEX HOUSE' can be seen beaming brightly across fashionable Central Park.

A hotel may seem a strange place for a child to grow up in but to me it's normal, and the long hallways make excellent tracks for racing my tricycle, making pit stops to say hello to the maids as they gossip around the linen closet.

When my father brings me a ballet costume back from a trip to Cuba, I can't wait to show it to my friend the 'Silver Queen' who works in the magazine shop. She is astonished to see a little fairy with wired wings descend from 1014 and pirouette among the glossy magazines and newsprint. The costume comes with a magic wand. I now feel prepared for all eventualities. I have magic and beauty.

I'm enrolled in Ecole Française, a fashionable Catholic school on East 53rd Street, and a bitter day comes when amid tears and clinging I'm torn from my mother. The front door of the school closes, she walks down the street and with each step she takes my heart cracks. I'm left alone in the cold stone church. I look at the marble statues of the saints and long for my mother.

But I grow to like school. We wear blue smocks and black stockings and every morning we enter through the green wooden doors and climb the staircase where the headmistress, Madamoiselle Guylem stands tank-like at the head of the stairs, greeting each student as she arrives. I bob a curtsey. 'Bonjour, Mademoiselle', I say, noticing how her feet puff over the edges of her shoes, like little pillows stuffed in boxes.

I make friends and play queen and her court at recess: 'Now you be the knight and come rescue me . . .'

At Christmas there is a pageant, a nativity play and one year I play the Virgin Mary and sit silent while rows of angels stand in the aisles singing Christmas Carols.

In the spring we twirl round a maypole on the ends of coloured ribbons and I learn to read and love books and can't draw and don't care and am whipped when I won't eat and am caught with liver and string beans in my pocket.

Every morning the school bus comes to collect me and every morning the children sing Happy Birthday, a ritual I have inaugurated. I invent talismans, symbols, the number 3. My reality is never a composite of past experience, but can be found only in the concentrated now. 'It's not your birthday,' my father says.

When I am eight, and suffering from anaemia, mother decides New York City isn't a healthy environment in which to bring up a child and that I need fresh air and country life. We duly move to a large estate in Westchester County. The house of stone and shingle is built on three levels, in acres of rolling lawns and landscaped gardens, and its back walls of solid glass look out on to a silver-birch forest that is floodlit at night to create a scenic fairyland.

We sit in the formal pink dining room, the walls of crushed mother-of-pearl, the table settings of gold plate gleaming in the candlelight, being served by Thompson, the one-eyed butler from England, who often misses me out while serving because he can only see half the table and our Southern cook, Margie, whose mood can only be ascertained by the volume of the crashing of pots and pans; and who talks to the food, the refrigerator, the stove and herself nonstop.

Boo Boetticher is my best friend. We go to the same ballet school and share some common fantasies. On cold winter afternoons we go deep into the woods to a little pond frozen to ice. We take off all our clothes and put on ballet costumes, little scraps of tulle and sequins, pale pastel drifts of gauze, and then like nymphs glide out on to the ice and dance under the white sky in the silent wood, watched only by a small grey squirrel.

Peter carries a bull whip. He is fifteen to my twelve, a large handsome boy. One day as we walk in the woods with our dogs he grabs me and pushing me against a tree tries to kiss me; to touch me 'there'. I hit him so hard with the stick I'm carrying that it breaks over his arm and I run and run till I'm out of breath, consumed with shame and the fear he will tell my mother on me, as if I'm somehow the guilty one.

His father's never at home and he and his brother and sister are more or less brought up by the butler who is hand-on-hip camp and always shouting 'Y'all get back in this house' to no avail. When we first moved in, his mother had come to welcome my mother and sat drunk on the sofa with ice cream running down her chin, her eyes unfocussed, and later in the week set her house on fire and died.

As we skate some of the neighbourhood boys, led by Peter, steal our clothes and run off with them. Humiliated we're forced to teeter down the country roads to Boo's house on our skates, shivering in our skimpy costumes till we find her older brother and he catches Peter and fights him and we get our clothes back and our mothers never know.

In the summer I go to Camp Owaisa in Massachusetts, where we live in log cabins like pioneers and Indians on Lake Adirondack in the Berkshire mountains. We spend our days divided into teams playing volleyball, softball, and tennis. We go swimming and boating. There are nature walks through lacy ferns where we catch velvety orange salamanders and chameleons to see them change colour; and I make an ashtray for my mother in pottery class.

Our days are strictly regulated, graphed out on clipboards by counsellors with muscular legs and hearty voices who blow whistles on lanyards and get us 'up and at 'em' from reveille to taps. I love camp. It's like having a whole family of sisters to play with, to confide in whispers after 'lights out', borrow each other's sweaters and never feel lonely.

At home I often eat alone. My parents go out a lot. Evenings at the theatre, fashionable restaurants: 21, the Stork Club. They have a box at the opera and enjoy the gala opening nights. I ask the maid to sit with me while I eat, to keep me company but she always refuses saying, 'No, Miss, it isn't proper'. But at camp we all eat together in the noisy wooden dining room, at rows of long tables. With all the fresh mountain air, sunshine and outdoor life we develop hearty appetites and attack our food with gusto. Platters of meat, bowls of steaming vegetables, baskets full of thick hunks of bread and pitchers of milk are passed up and down the table while we keep up a steady stream of chatter, eating, laughing, comparing suntans and teasing our counsellor Joanie about her fiancé Lenny who works at our brother camp Adirondack.

I am awake in the middle of the night. I can see our cubbyholes with our shorts and T-shirts, the rows of beds and hear the girls breathing beside me. A patch of moonlight lies on the blanket. I hear the buzz of a mosquito. He circles me closer and closer. I lie silent and watch. I've never seen one so close. He hovers over my arm and lands. He stands in a forest of hair, drills into the soft flesh and drinks while I observe him.

The last night of summer is the awards ceremony. I win awards for best all-round water sports, for water skiing, and tennis tournament mixed doubles. Then we all go down to the lake in a solemn procession carrying candles on boards on which we have each written a wish. The whole camp stands at the edge of the lake, faces illuminated as they set their candles on to the water.

I walk alone to a point above the lake where a bench is carved out of the rock under a willow tree. I sit and look at the little lights as they float under the stars on the water. Voices rise like mist from the lake below and float on the mild summer's air. I suddenly realize that when I die everything will go on, the wooden dining room will ring with laughter and the clatter of plates. At summer's end, candles will be floated on the lake and their flickering lights will mimic the stars lying on their smooth basalt arc. Another child will sit here but I will be gone. Already I feel like a ghost.

CHAPTER 2

My parents have an aversion to organized religion. It embarrasses and puzzles them that I am constantly ducking into churches.

I wander in the empty cathedral among the saints, the Stations of the Cross, the guttering candles and gaze into the dizzy spin of spires vaulting upward as if to pierce heaven itself. I delight in the stained-glass windows of luscious rubies, topaz and sapphire ice. In the third row is the click of a rosary and the mumble of prayers that slip from beneath the bent head of an old woman. I stand transfixed before the blanched marble statue of Christ, who fills me with such a powerful longing, contracting my heart in so painful a sweetness, it sends me home in secret to burn my clothes.

* * * *

Fourteenth Year. After school, sitting in the garden with a plate of Oreo cookies and a glass of milk; a gentle breeze tumbles showers of gold among leaves; there is the buzz of a lawnmower and the sweet smell of new-mown grass. Nearby my mother is weeding in the rock garden and from the kitchen the sound of water as the vegetables for supper are being washed. Carefully I take the Oreo apart and with my teeth scrape off the rich cream centre, then balance the sweetness with a swallow of cold milk. Using this formula I am contentedly working my way through the plate when suddenly like music in a minor key, fear strikes and I feel the day drain away. Balanced between the known and the abyss of the unconscious, I teeter on the thin rim of every day, dragging my swollen shadow. I run to my mother: 'I'm afraid' – of death!

My mother is kind, patient. She reassures me that when we die we will go to a place called heaven. As she describes it, it sounds amazingly like the house she wants to build. She begins to decorate it with French antiques in pastel shades, even adding vases of her favourite 'American Beauty' roses.

I realize that she doesn't know. It is wishful thinking, not knowledge.

I go on strike, a sly secret rebellion. At fifteen I am counter. I do badly at school – no, not badly. I do nothing. All systems are below contempt. All the histories tried and found wanting. Momentous battles neatly numbered into 1642-1812-1914. Mr G. in English Lit. is busy murdering long-dead poets; taking apart each line, beat and hexameter; telling us what to think it means till all the juice is as dry as the chalk on the blackboard. Anyway, I am too busy trekking through Africa or sailing the vast seas to the edge of the world to notice. At lunch in the cafeteria, buried in a book, I walk down Joyce's Dublin streets and possibilities arise beyond the confining school room. After recess I am often the first man into Tibet.

On Saturdays I escape to the movies with my best friend Mar. We hang out at the dim Art Deco palaces. We want a life with a soundtrack. We want to look like Kim Novak as 'Jeanne Eagles'; like Garbo in anything, like the models in the make-up ads in the drugstore windows. We check out our cheekbones in the mirrors over the candy machines.

We go to Mar's house to have our serious talks, as she can lock her bedroom door. We sneak up to her room past her mother sitting drunk in the stale living room. Her father is in the army and has a grey crew cut and never comes home. We try to avoid her brother but he leaps out at us with a whoopee cushion making obscene noises which we try disdainfully to ignore before dissolving in a fit of giggles. Little Jimmy, who twenty years later will walk into the lake to drown himself, his arm full of needle tracks, dances around us like a little blond elf. Mar is laughing and chewing on a mouthful of Sen Sens to disguise the fact that she's been smoking all afternoon.

We discuss our latest passion, bullfighting, the *corrida*. We execute passes. 'Heh, toro!' stamp our feet. We are aficionados. We like the lean mean *torreros*, Manolete in his 'suit of lights' – death in the afternoon. We lie across her bed. James Dean stares down from the wall. I stare back. I love him. I am him.

We adopt our hero's uniform; rebel jeans, the black shirts of the Beats. 'Where are you going dressed like that?!' exasperated mother; innocently, 'Like what? Everyone dresses like this.' It would seem her everybody and my everybody have never met.

The boys at school are divided into two classes, the 'nice' boys, meaning rich and the 'others', meaning Italian. At expensive parties meant to introduce us to society we cha-cha stiffly with sweaty palmed boys under striped marquees, past swans carved out of ice and filled with caviar.

Flowers arrive. I go with rich men's sons in chauffeur-driven cars, into the city, to night clubs, with orchid corsages like exotic spiders strapped to my wrist. I go on weekends at prep schools, Choate, Andover, and Peddie with boys I want to avoid kissing.

Rocky, a boy from my school, invites me to a football game. He is the handsomest boy in town and a senior, leader of the pack; a blue-eyed Italian with the soul of a garage mechanic.

My father catches me as I am going out the door to meet him. He flies into a rage and beats me, smacking my head hard against the wall, shouting something about $2. I am sure he'll kill me. My crime is my lost student pass, but I sense this punishment lies deeper, primal and unspoken.

I arrive at the game, my head aching, my face swollen, but Rocky doesn't meet me at the gate as arranged. At school the next day he avoids me and nothing is ever mentioned at home either.

We move back to the city as the drive to Westchester is too much for my father who has had a heart attack. My parents give me a sweet sixteen party at the Plaza where

I wear a dream of a white organza ballgown scalloped in pink moire. Harry Belafonte performs. At tables cluttered with crystal and silver women lean forward enthralled, their exposed breasts hanging over half-eaten steaks. A superb blonde pouts over the rim of her champagne glass hungrily eyeing the smooth caramel skin, the shirt open to the waist, while her balding husband sits twirling bourbon in a squat glass, feeling vaguely threatened. 'Sure is a hell of a good-looking man, for a Negro,' he admits.

My mother has her heart set on my marrying Gordon, the nephew of Sir Isaac Wolfson. She tells me a few hundred times about the party he gave in Monte Carlo and who was there. Her descriptive powers concentrate on what they own, their fortunes of paper, cloth, and meat; colossal empires built on sweat and cunning; the worth of a man scale-weighted with dollar signs. My ambitions lie elsewhere.

In 1959 I stay briefly with my piano teacher on unfashionable 100th Street in a large apartment filled with books, music and intense intellectual discussion. Sonia Stockheim has been a concert pianist, protégé of Rachmaninov, and given it up to teach children like me, who don't practise.

On the weekends Mar comes to the city and we hang out in Greenwich Village on West Fourth Street, in cafes like the Fat Black Cat and Figaro's, on the lookout for interesting people. When we find any we follow them to see what they will do, where they go. We are the spies of lives. We trail one white-haired man who turns out to be the artist William De Kooning and takes us to the

Cedar Bar. Another man turns out to be a murderer newly released from prison and looking for sex.

While Mar smokes and drinks black coffee and I eat we discuss the lives of our heroes, which interest us even more than their work. We especially like the lives of tragic genius – the more tragic the better. We are fascinated by decadence, but at a suburban distance.

We haunt the shrines of our heroes. We screw up our courage and knock on Roy Schatt's door. He's a famous photographer and was a close friend of James Dean. We want to see the chair where Jimmy sat, see his photographs of Marilyn Monroe without make-up on the wall. Unbelievably he invites us in and unbelievably we tell him we are going to be actresses. He offers to give us acting lessons and takes us as his students.

Many afternoons are spent on Sutton Place; sitting on my bed listening to America: the raw-boned songs of Appalachia, Woodie Guthrie, the clear-water voice of Joan Baez.

It's the time of the Newport Folk Festival and we absolutely have to go, so we tell each set of parents we are staying at the other's house and jump on the train to hear nightfuls of wonderful music, ride on the back of motorcycles of some nice Hell's Angels and sleep on the beach.

When my father finds out he's furious and makes me break off the friendship. Each set of parents believes the other's child is the bad influence.

Again, the question of college. We are sitting in my mother's dressing room with its silk moire hangings. On tiny feet a gold filigree tray is carrying its treasure of perfume across the Venetian-glass dressing-table. Joy, Dior, Nuit de Noël, all the odours of Grasse, gums of Arabia, sex of exotic animals lie evaporating in faceted containers of crystal. While we discuss college my mother is showing me how to put on make-up. There are jars of colour; 'Touch and Glow', they promise, and pencils and brushes; a swansdown powder puff, its pink tendrils aquiver as it listens to our conversation. 'The secret, darling, is to blend. Now I wear a lot of make-up, more than most, but it looks natural because I blend. Always up; all the lines of the face must go up.'

It's the same old story. My parents want me to go to college. I want to 'live'. 'You can "live" after college,' she says as she circles my eyes with black.

'Anyway,' I continue, 'I'm thinking of becoming a nun.'

'You need some more colour on your lips,' she adds, applying a cherry-red lipstick.

I look in the mirror and I don't recognize myself.

'Just beautiful,' my mother says proudly.

I suck in my cheeks and pose like the models in *Vogue*.

'Don't wrinkle your forehead,' she warns.

Later at night, when I wash off the make-up, I watch as my face disappears down the drain.

Of course I go to college. I audition for and win a place at Carnegie Tech. It has the best drama school in the country, noted for turning out solid Shakespearean actors.

For my audition I crouch on top of the desk like a kitten and do Shaw's Cleopatra and a piece I write myself about a young Jewish boy, a child in Auschwitz during the Second World War. I grow thin, my head is shaved. I try to wrap my ragged clothes to my pitiful little body. The plight of this little boy touches something in me and I see myself in him.

For whatever reason I'm accepted and go to Pittsburgh in early September, but I am certainly not the stuff of which great actresses are made. The shock of watching myself unnerves me. In class I lose my voice. The speech teacher even asks me what country I come from. I'm called to the dean's office where Ted Hoffman sighs, 'You won't make it through on your looks alone.' I retreat hurt to the botanical gardens.

*   *   *   *

In the summer of '61 my parents send me to Sarah Lawrence summer school in Florence to be 'finished'. We live high in the hills above the city in the Tore de Bellosguardo, eating our pasta in Renaissance opulence. We spend our days inside the cool museums among fabulous art, and outside in the bigger museum that is Florence itself. We learn Italian, say *Firenze*, and walk like Beatrice along the Arno as it flows thickly under the Ponte Vecchio. In the little wooden shops which line the bridge we slip thin silver rings with opaque stones on our fingers, stretch our hands in the light air and buy nothing. My room-mate, Marie, who speaks her Italian with a Texas accent falls in love with Michelangelo's statue of David so we sit in the Piazza in the afternoons gazing at him. I make do with a prince. Out of vanity he doesn't wear his glasses and drives into a statue in the town square.

We go on a school outing to Assisi, home of St Francis. We queue to see the flat Giottos, St Clair's Church, with her golden hair lying in a glass case, and the blackened finger of some saint, holy relic encased in gold pointing heavenward. At sunrise, unable to sleep, I go to the monastery. In the courtyard where the sun is laying its first tracks, a very young monk, beautiful as an angel, stands in a halo of light sweeping out the church. I feel he possesses some wonderful secret I long to know. For the rest of the summer lying in the dry buzzing grass or walking in the formal gardens of the villa I think about him.

One night I wake in a fever, my body aching. Even the furniture in the room has become painful. A doctor is called. I'm moved to a nursing home run by nuns. The Sisters of Mercy, I give no mercy. I torture them with questions about Christ which they evade by smoothing the sheets and plumping the pillows. *Mio dottore* arrives. It's mononucleosis. The next day, worried, he hurries in to say it's leukaemia. By the afternoon it is reduced to anaemia. My Italian and his English don't seem to gel. If I am going to die, I reason, I might as well see Paris first.

The nuns squeak and flap their coifs in the hallways as I leave for the station. It's true I feel a little giddy, but I'm determined and by the time I arrive in Paris I've forgotten about being sick.

Paris is carved out of light. Light gushes out of the mouths of fountains and floods the avenues and promenades. It streams down the dome of Sacré Coeur and drips on to the bronze horses as they drink along the bridges. It is a polar light so radiantly beautiful against the night that the stars become ashamed and retreat.

Multiple stairs lean against the Butte where I take the first small hotel I find. Doors bang, footsteps in the hall, drunken laughter, the handle of my door is tried several times. For a few hours I think it's a party.

The next morning I make a better arrangement and set out to explore the city. For several days I wander the antique streets, criss-crossing ancient bridges and quays. I live in the cafés stirring cups of bitter coffee and of course I fall in love. I discover Shakespeare and Company across from Nôtre Dame, the meeting place for young artists, writers and students. I quickly become a member of the group. At night we go to the Champs Elysée, where the artists draw elaborate pictures on the sidewalk. We sing and pass the hat before going to Les Halles where we eat up all the francs we've collected.

The companion of the streets? Anglo-Irish Dublin boy, blue-eyed and insolent. We are on Vert Galant when, on a whim, I say 'I love you, Michael Reynolds'. The moment I say it, it becomes true.

September 3, 1961, Paris is not a place to remain sober. For my nineteenth birthday I decide to get drunk. Michael and I celebrate with friends in an Algerian restaurant where I begin with beer. I pass out almost immediately and Michael has to carry me home where I revive and rage and rant and run around like a mad person. I find myself pounding on a mirror and hearing a voice shouting something about truth; I realize it's mine.

Michael drags me up the stairs still shouting and holds me in his arms till I stop shouting and struggling and fall asleep. I scare him now. When I wake up the next morning, he is looking down at me, his eyes distant. 'How do you feel?' he asks. 'Fine; why?' I answer. Then I remember. 'What happened?' I ask. 'It's not important,' he says. But, he is packing. I don't understand. I wonder what I did, what I said. He won't talk about it and leaves later in the day.

I wander around St Germain and stand on bridges and look into the Seine. Night drains into dawn. The moon hangs exhausted in a tree. As I walk down Boulevard St Michel I see a large brown bear being led along the street by a gypsy. The bear has what appears to be a skirt around his waist patterned in green and pink triangles. On his head a pointed hat, decorated with sequins. I stop in front of them and the gypsy begins to play the concertina. '*Dansez*,' he cracks and the bear rises up on his hind legs lumbering backwards and forwards, his coat dusty, his eyes uncomprehending. I give them all of my francs. I won't need them. It is time to go home to America.

*   *   *   *

I become a model. A perfect illusion trapped in mirrors full of cameras. Inventing myself again, I paint on myself. My lips I enamel with the juice of rubies.

It's while showing ballgowns at Saks Fifth Avenue that I'm seen by Oleg Cassini. He asks me to model his collection, and also to have dinner with him. My mother is delighted, but first he must meet my father.

He calls for me and he and my father sit in the living room having a drink and making small talk. Oleg, silver-haired, strenuously elegant seems at ease as he sips his cocktail. I am a nervous wreck. I always feel personally responsible for any flaws a person might exhibit when introduced to my parents.

Oleg is older than my father and has been the lover, husband and escort to many famous beauties; married to Jean Tierney and engaged to Grace Kelly before she became HSH Princess Grace of Monaco. He's come a long way from his youth when he'd come to New York from Italy and lived at the YMCA. A top couturier and man about town, now he designs all of Jackie Kennedy's clothes when she is First Lady.

He passes the test and we go out, usually to supper and then to Le Club where we dance the Twist, often joined by his brother Igor, the columnist Cholly Knickerbocker.

We go to the theatre with the producer Ray Stark and have drinks with Salvador Dali at the St Regis. People are always coming over to our table to say hello and be introduced. Powerful older men, but I noticed how they stare at my figure and try to look down my dress.

On a Thursday when Oleg sends his car to pick me up I'm taken to his home, where he greets me in a silk dressing gown, an ascot at his neck. We aren't going out, he tells me; 'I thought it would be nice to have dinner at home for a change.' I'm not so sure. He had prepared a light supper and handing me a glass of champagne leaves me in front of the television set. I'm nervous at dinner as I've never been alone with him. Before I even have a chance to finish my dessert, he picks me up in his arms and starts to carry me towards the bedroom. This is far beyond where I want to go and seeing the expression on my face stops him. 'You really are afraid, aren't you,' he says. I'm still very innocent and he's a gentleman and leaves it at that.

At about the same time at a poetry course at the New School, I meet the young poet Gerard Malanga. At least he certainly looks like a poet – a face usually seen on Greek statues, and like a statue he has the courage of silence. He spends an entire weekend at my parent's country house in Westport lying by the swimming pool and saying nothing. At the dinner table the strain is unbearable as my parents try to make polite conversation and he answers in monosyllables. He takes me to Andy Warhol's Factory where Paul Morrisey videos me and I watch myself on the TV doing nothing for a long time, which Andy likes.

Having a coffee after class one evening, he takes a ring from his finger and gives it to me. 'I don't want your ring,' I say. 'It isn't that way.' But he insists I wear it, so I take it and forget about it, till a week later when a letter arrives from the well-known avant-garde film maker Willard Maas. In the letter he accuses me of beguiling this young boy into giving me a ring which he in fact had given him. As I could not possibly understand Gerard, I should return the ring and never see him again. I begin to suspect there are forms of love I don't know about yet.

Rather half-heartedly I have continued taking acting lessons and my teacher Pat introduces me to the director Phoebe Brand who is casting a Lorca play for Circle in the Square. In her dressing room at the theatre she and Pat watch me in the mirror as we speak. They exchange looks and decide I will be perfect for the lead, making me wonder what Pat has told her.

We begin rehearsals. I'm terrible! Phoebe is maternal

and keeps reassuring me I'm fine. I become more and more panic-stricken and as opening night approaches I'm absolutely sick with anxiety. I have nightmares. I'm on stage. I've forgotten my lines. I open my mouth, I stand paralyzed before the audience. At a dress rehearsal my mother comes to watch and takes me and my costume to Miss Bitz, her dressmaker, where she lowers the neckline to a fraction below decency and gives me an unbreathable waist. When Phoebe sees it on opening night she is furious, but I am beyond caring. I only hope I can remember my lines and get through it, before I go off some place to die. Never again, I tell myself!

It begins. I move my arms. I put one foot in front of the other and imitate walking. Like this I move across the stage. I hear myself read the line, 'blacker than the hearts of some of the women' as 'blacker than some of the women'. The leading man looks at his hand, his jaw twitches. At the end there is applause. Perhaps they are trying to wake themselves up. In spite of my obvious lack of talent, I am noticed by Fred Zinneman who's interested in putting me in the movies and asks me to prepare a scene for him. 'No Shakespeare,' he says.

CHAPTER 3

On Easter Sunday, my father brings home a gigantic box of Perugina candy, a dozen 'American Beauty' roses for my mother and a nosegay of violets for me and takes his 'girls' to brunch at the Hampshire House. Massive arrangements of Easter lilies bank the beautiful pale grey dining room, and baskets of coloured Easter eggs and milk chocolate rabbits decorate the tables. The room smells of whisky and flowers and delicious food. Easter Sunday brunch is a tradition in New York and reservations have been made well in advance for what is practically a private party.

Eleanor Lefcourt is there with her husband who owns Château Martin Wine. 'Hello, you gorgeous things,' she says in her smoky voice as she kisses the air beside our cheeks. Across the room Harry Frischling, who owns a detective agency and must know half the secrets of New York, is with Amy Edwards, XXXX, reputed to be a Mafia chief is sitting in a corner with his wife, a former beauty queen, and Father Flanagan, a Jesuit, who goes everywhere with them, and nearby Dr Maxwell Maltz, the plastic surgeon, is not speaking to Betty who is feeding slivers of chicken to her toy poodle Mozel. Zsa Zsa Gabor is sitting two tables away talking nonstop as usual. Ralph Bellamy, the actor, stops by to say hello. 'Sam, you lucky devil! How come you've got two beautiful women?' 'Skill, not luck!' my father grins, putting down his Bloody Mary to shake hands.

At the next table, a spray of diamonds trembles on the silk blouse of a Park Avenue matron. 'That's nothing,' whispers a friend. 'You should see what her husband had to give his mistress to keep her mouth shut.'

There is a fashion show and a prize for the most beautiful hat. Pat, a friend of my mother's, wins with a hat loaded down with at least half a florist shop entwined with enough fruit for an agricultural exhibition. Applause sprinkles the room as she goes up to collect her magnum of Moët et Chandon. Within earshot two bitches are talking: 'My dear, she must be older than God, why she's had so many face lifts she looks positively Chinese!' 'Darling!!' they squeal in unison as she passes their table. By 3 pm white kid gloves lie deflated on tables as women take out gold compacts and retouch their still perfect make-up.

After lunch there is the Easter Parade. All of New York society strolls along Fifth Avenue to St Patrick's Cathedral and Rockefeller Center. As we leave the Hampshire House I take my father's arm and squeeze it. 'Thank you for the brunch, Daddy, and my violets.'

When we get to Fifth Avenue we can see the huge Festival of Love that is going on in the park. Young girls, noble as queens without a court, are walking with their boyfriends, barefoot saints with beards. I think they are so beautiful, but my mother disapproves. 'I wouldn't mind,' she says, 'if they at least combed their hair.'

Uncaring of her opinion, they lie in the grass like delicious animals sunning their haunches. Pan is playing his flute, standing under a tree with flowers in his hair. He has many pretty followers, young bacchantes with stars and crescents tattooed on their cheeks arrive from Queens, their ankle bells tinkling as they pour out of the subway.

For certain there will be a chemical reaction. Diamonds will melt. The dark blue face of the east like a raincloud turns slowly toward the west.

* * * *

In 1963 I marry Marc Morrel. Sitting in the Fat Black Cat I notice a beautiful young man with eyes so clear you can see through them staring at me. He looks down. His hand moves over the paper. He is drawing me. With a few fine lines he captures me. Descendant of General Custer, the Indian fighter, long-haired, an artist, impoverished of course. Wonderful credentials. My parents are not in the mood to agree, so we run away together and I become momentarily an orphan.

We live happily together in a huge loft in Chinatown. I collect pets. A white cat called Cat, a parrot, my miniature Dachshund, Sappho, a tank of tropical fish, and of course Charlie. One day, when Marc and I are visiting the monkey house, admiring their antics and chatting with the keeper, he asks if I would like a Capuchin monkey. 'Yes!' I say. 'No!' says Marc. So Charlie comes to stay. Unfortunately Charlie is a little on the neurotic side. He screams at the top of his lungs and throws tantrums and his food. He steals things and his toilet habits leave a lot to be desired.

*   *   *   *

In the 60s, borders which never existed are crossed. Acids slide open the panels of the mind, eating through the partitions of 'should be' and the doors of perception unlock as the mind registers what the eyes had always seen and the heart has always known.

The House of God stands empty. The doors are locked in the daytime now, while inside priests in glamorous robes are serving up a fine theatre replete with kneelings and crossings. In this age God comes to the streets. He is walking in the fields among the wheat. Pilgrims, poets, prophets, saints, and madmen travel the lifeways. They come from California, from Liverpool, from India and Amsterdam. They come singing in strange languages about truth, about peace, about love.

A swami in saffron robes preaches in a store front on the Lower East Side in a thick Bengali accent and *kartals*[*] tinkle on the concrete streets from Delhi to Moscow.

In the 60s, we take over the universities, where they teach nothing, sit-in at Berkeley and NYU. We squat on the slum lords and abolish money, though we spend a lot of it. We are beautiful, our bodies perfumed with essential oils, with musk and jasmine, incense and opium. Our hair grows wild as woods and raw herbs. We are

* Sacred hand cymbals used in devotional music.

skinned in psychedelic gypsy silks, in jeans and beads. We live in geodesic domes in the redwood forests, as tribes in tepees. We live with Hesse, Watts and Leary, with Siddhartha and Guatama, with the Bardo and Zen, Op art, Pop art, At 'Be Ins', 'Love Ins', 'Happenings', we turn on, tune in, drop out, and we free love.

A few months after Marc and I are married I become pregnant. My appetite, always good becomes enormous. Every afternoon I go downstairs to the pastry shop on the corner and buy a large birthday cake decorated with pink roses and devour the whole thing for an afternoon snack. Eventually the girl behind the counter stops asking me if I want an inscription.

It's no small wonder my son weighs 10½ lb, on St Patrick's Day, 1964, when they paint the white line down the middle of Fifth Avenue green and the parade passes under my hospital window as he is being born. I am reading Sartre, so we name him Jean-Paul.

The nurses tell me I have the most beautiful baby in the hospital, and the biggest. They bring him in and lay him reverently in my arms. I am terrified. While the other mothers coo and look at tiny hands and feet, I lie paralyzed, watching him sleep till I develop pins and needles and the nurse comes and takes him away.

Death is the midwife at every birth. In every meeting leaving, at the end of every pleasure, pain. I am empty now, my sad belly hangs defeated. I have grown bones and blood, have created a living passage of my body from one world to another, but we are separate. The cord is cut. Now you curl a trusting hand around my finger, are comforted with lullabies and nourished by kisses. I smell your forehead of talc and honey.

My little mousie with your toothless grin. My little yellow duck with apple sauce on your cheeks. Sleep now, in your crib watched over by a plush bunny and a Raggedy Andy from grandpa, sleep in the plump envelope of your skin with its familiar features.

*   *   *   *

In the studio Phil Ochs pushes back his chair from the table, picks up his guitar and sings 'I ain't marchin any more' . . . and laughs.

Years later he will be silent as we sit in Max's Kansas City having a drink together. He has been garrotted by thieves in a freight yard in South America. They break his voice and his mind. He hangs himself a week later. But tonight he laughs as he tells us a story about Bob Dylan while fishing in the deep pockets of his coat for his notebook and scraps of songs.

We pick at the remains of a spaghetti dinner while planning 'the War is Over' peace march, when I am interrupted by a call from Rap Brown, leader of the Black Panthers.

On the day of the parade, we march from the Village to the UN carrying placards saying 'the War is Over', shouting jubilantly. 'It's over. The war is over. No more war!' Laughing and dancing through the streets our gaiety is infectious and thousands join us hoping that by saying no to war they will somehow force peace to break out.

By the autumn of '66 America is on the greatest peace march in history. From all over the country they come to Washington, DC to confront the masters of war. Sons of slaves, daughters of the American Revolution, Indians in feathered bonnets and beads, Vietnam veterans, students and hippies, rich and poor. All religions, races and creeds. A rainbow of people protesting injustice.

In the bright sunlight I photograph the American dream. Through the lens of my Nikon I see a long-haired boy going to the doors of the Pentagon with a petition. Halfway up the steps the soldiers attack him, beating him mercilessly with their clubs till blood streams down his face. I lower my camera, the picture untaken.

The soldiers order us to leave. They try to move us on, but we have a permit to be there. 'Sit down,' I shout. They line up, these order-followers, with their jack-boots, their guns and tear gas, but 'we shall not be moved'; 'We shall overcome'. Brutishly, unthinking, they move forward like a well-oiled machine. They roll over us clubs swinging, flinging pain and wounding; dispersing us.

That evening in a bar we watch the 6 o'clock news as it reports on the march and the unprovoked attack on the soldiers.

We're having a beer and talking about the day's events when the owner comes over. 'Y'all better git. They's a buncha guys from the Klan comin' down the street and they ain' partial to no long-haired commie queers.' Lickety split we're out the back door, into the car and slamming down the highway towards New York.

* * * *

In the winter of '67 Marc's first one-man show opens to acclaim at the prestigious Radich Gallery on Madison Avenue. Dennis Hopper drops by to look at the work, a series of sculptures using the American flag and talk about a film he's working on, which will be *Easy Rider*. Soon after the opening police raid the gallery and close the show, arresting Stephen Radich, the owner, and charging him with desecration of the American flag.

It will take many years in a case defended by the Civil Liberties Union before Marc and the gallery are finally vindicated by the Supreme Court, but museums and galleries withdraw their offers and it finishes off the gallery.

Soon after the raid on the gallery *Life* magazine comes to the studio photographing and interviewing Marc, calling him the leader of the 'New Left', which makes me smile. I know Marc doesn't know what the 'New Left' is, or the 'Old Left' for that matter. Marc isn't political – eccentric yes, sending back bills with 'deceased' written on the envelope or stamping pictures of Mickey Mouse and Donald Duck in his passport – but he isn't political. He is simply an artist mirroring the times he is living in.

It is not politics but romantic glamour that leads us to make a documentary film about Che Guevara, shooting it to look like news footage but using actors who resemble the main characters interspersed with actual news photos. The film ends in Bolivia with Che's death and luckily the foliage in Central Park is similar enough to shoot the guerrilla scenes.

Not long after the Bay of Pigs, on a sunny Sunday, the light being good, armed with toy guns, camouflage-suited, bearded and looking like Cuban guerrillas we take the bus uptown to film. We make our way through the tangled commotion of the city to Fifth where we pass the windows of Bergdorf Goodman showing the latest beaded micro skirts, and then into the park. People stare but then people always stare.

The filming goes well and pleased we retire to an outdoor café and are happily eating gazpacho when the police arrive in answer to calls saying that the revolution has begun and Cuba has invaded New York.

Castro invites us to visit Cuba, but at 2 o'clock one morning in the early spring I wake Marc to say 'Let's go live in Paris'. At the time of the Chicago riots during the Democratic Convention we are at sea on a student ship bound for Paris. Phil Ochs writes 'Where were you in Chicago' . . . and says it's about us.

*   *   *   *

The white winter sky ventures too low over Paris and finds itself impaled on the spires of Nôtre Dame. A *clochard* sits oblivious in the warmth of the Metro at République as the trains come and go through the afternoon tunnels, but the workers are still faithful to the cafés full of strong coffees and deep liquors.

A bad-tempered wind is racketing around the courtyard outside the studio. Thirty-two degrees fahrenheit and I am cooking the inevitable spaghetti dinner, wearing my coat, a scarf wound round my head and mittens. Incurable romantics we had rented a studio made of glass in the centre of Paris. It is impossible to heat.

But Paris is as always a 'moveable feast'. My agent Dorian Leigh comes to pick us up in a noble old Rolls-Royce and takes us to lunch at a Hungarian restaurant and makes us welcome. Eating a thick goulash and drinking champagne we talk about the modelling scene. In order to open her agency on Rue Malakoff Dorian had had to fight the French government who believed modelling agencies were prostitution rackets. She had convinced them otherwise and singlehandedly changed the laws of France. 'Well, my grandmother was the sheriff back in Texas,' she laughs. An exquisite black and white blue-eyed beauty she and her sister Suzy Parker had been top models for years before Suzy went to Hollywood and Dorian to Paris.

Our notoriety has preceded us, prompting her to tell us, 'I was a communist, too, when I was young.' We don't bother to explain any more, that we are not communists.

Dorian puts me to work right away sending me to *Vogue* magazine where I meet the great fashion photographer Henry Clarke who asks me, 'Would you like to go to Spain with me for *Vogue*?'

* * * *

Inquisition black, its men as dangerous as the *arrucina* of the *corrida*, Toledo hangs like an El Greco above the plain, stretched upwards and yearning like St Teresa of Avila. On a cliff, outside a monastery with massive wooden doors, on a wintry afternoon, I pose in bathing suits, lying on rocks, their small indentations filled with frozen water. In the courtyard of the Alhambra wearing three sets of false eyelashes and two hairpieces thirty-six poses are clicked out by the camera, watched by the ghosts of the women of the harem who look down from the windows of the seraglio.

My career progresses rapidly till it reaches the apex which is for every model a cover on either *Harper's Bazaar* or *Vogue*. At the agency in Milan, Giorgio tells me I have been booked for the cover of *Harper's Bazaar*.

I'm so excited I get up at 5 am and carefully begin glueing on false eyelashes one by one with the precision of a Swiss clock-maker. I want to be absolutely perfect. I am brushing out my hair when an English model comes into the dressing room unloading her heavy bags. 'Hi!' I say. 'What are you doing?' she asks. 'The cover,' I say. 'But I was booked for the cover,' she exclaims. We sit side by side and measure our beauty against each other, unsure now we note the flaws and failures of our features, hold a magnifying mirror to our insecurities. 'What a bunch of bastards,' she says. It isn't till the magazine is on the newsstands that I find out they have used me.

That night to amuse ourselves a group of us go to the circus. We dress up for the event. I wear Renaissance velvets and boots. My pal Barry McKinley, the 6'2" red-headed Australian photographer is enveloped in a rac-coon coat, while Eva, one of Helmut Newton's Swedish models, whose Italian husband likes to beat her, favours black leather. A pretty male model tags along. In the car Eva takes a thin joint out of her purse, rolls it between her fingers and offers me a hit.

We're late and the circus has begun. As we go down the aisle, the spotlight is turned on us and the crowd applauds. It's a provincial circus, the audience local. High above, the trapeze artistes make difficult calcula-tions on metal swings. At the roar of a lion the little boy sitting next to me gasps in terror and grabs the hand of his grandfather, but it is an old lion who is put through his paces by his master. The lion-tamer flicks his whip.

The lion gets up on a box. The lion-tamer shouts. The lion gets down from the box.

In the ring a stocky little horse runs delightedly around the circle carrying on his back the lion-tamer's daughter. She is wearing a costume of tulle and sparkles and shows her beautiful legs encased in pink tights. Her coarse face smiles invitingly under a rhinestone tiara. Enthralled the little boy sees a princess. She will live in his psyche now, his princess sought among the girls he will meet and love.

A dwarf waddles forward and throws a bucket of confetti at us. His stunted legs run double time around a clown, a tall pierrot, a tear painted on his cheek. The dwarf scratches his behind. He falls down. The crowd laughs and stuffs candy in its mouth. In the tent's ceiling the tightrope walker plugs his pole into the solid air.

After the circus, the ringmaster comes to our seats bringing a tiny lion cub he wants to sell. I pet his sleepy face as he gnaws my knuckles. I'm tempted to buy him, but Barry talks me out of it.

In the road outside I take off my coat and throw it on the ground. I lie down and close my eyes. 'What are you doing?' Barry asks.

'I'm staying here. I don't want to go.'

'Where?'

'Back.'

*   *   *   *

At one hour into 1969 my husband's silver-headed cane leans against a table at the Café Flore, where we are drinking champagne to celebrate the New Year. From outside a cacophony of horns, hoots and shouts bursts into the café. We all go out to have a look and find a crowd of people marching down the Boulevard St Germain.

In the spirit of New Year's Eve we join in the celebration as it comes past the Flore. I dance along still holding a glass of champagne in my hand. *Bonne Année, Bonne Année*, Happy New Year! Behind me people fill the broad avenue and crush up on to the sidewalk. Cars are abandoned in the street, people standing on them shouting. Now I catch what they are really saying. It isn't *Bonne Année*. It's *Allez à l'Elysée*. They are marching against the government. As I realize this I turn to see a battalion of French police, *'le Flic'*, advancing toward us behind plastic shields. Marc grabs me and drags me down a side street. I run and run till I'm exhausted. Politics! I am sick of this dream which never wakes up.

* * * *

In 1969, they devalue the franc and being the sole support of the family I decide to join Askews, who are willing to pay me a lot of money, whether I work or not, and we come to live in London. I love riding above London and on the double-decker buses. Up the spiral staircase, swayed around the corners, top floor, front seat, best seat. I love long-haired London, Carnaby Street, miniskirted London, Liverpooled and Beatled London. I love the signs dotted around the city saying 'Take Courage', not realizing that Courage is a beer not an exhortation.

Marc and I go to Stonehenge for the Summer Solstice Festival. We sleep by the fire, near an encampment of tepees. Hauled up from the subconscious the great stone monolith broods under the night and keeps its secrets. In a warm sleeping bag the cold air balanced on my nose, it feels so good to lie against the ground, to feel the solid depth of the earth, safe from falling, to hear scraps of music and voices and people moving from campfire to campfire; safer than rooms behind doors. Before sunrise a solemn procession of Druids winds its way toward the great stones. Two young men formally dressed in pink faces and wing collars have set up a table topped with linen and candelabrum and sit pleasantly eating breakfast and toasting Stonehenge with champagne from a silver ice bucket as hippies in loin cloths wander by. We all wait expectantly for the sun to rise over Stonehenge, but when it rises, it is so cloudy no one can see it.

Valerie and Gloria Askew are wonderful to me. They introduce me to everyone and promote me so well that within a week I am booked solid.

The agency on Bruton Street is a mad house, with models, kids, cups of tea and dogs; the phones ringing constantly keeping the bookers on the hop. Mrs Askew, the mother, who is a psychic, predicts I will have a brilliant future; the poor bookkeeper who is always being hassled by the girls, the clients or both tells me, 'My last job was more peaceful.' 'Oh, what was that?' 'I was with the bomb disposal unit!'

One of the nicest photographers I work with is Justin de Villeneuve. I'm surprised he booked me as he only works with Twiggy. Justin insists I sit down and eat something before the shoot. He sends out for the most delicious food, tiny portions each served in its own dish, and hovers solicitously as I eat. Twiggy is playing billiards at the far end of the studio. She has a presence which makes me want to watch her.

On seamless paper, I turn, tilt back my head, feel the light ripple like water down my face. The strobes pop and flash. Justin comes from behind the camera. He kisses me gently on both cheeks. 'Beautiful, just beautiful.'

I'm working all the time now, supporting the family. 'Marc, I'm so exhausted,' I plead. 'If you go to the shops, I'll make the dinner.' 'You're the woman. You go to the shops!' is his answer. The phone rings, interrupting. It's my mother saying, 'Darling, please come.' She's crying. 'You're father has cancer, he's dying.'

I leave on the next plane for America and rush straight to the hospital to my father. I lean over his hospital bed to hug him and kiss his scratchy cheek. I've never seen him unshaven before. I notice pictures of myself cut from magazines on the night table of my father, who has never approved of my modelling.

The doctors had opened him up, seen the ravages of the disease, knew it was hopeless, and closed him up. Cancer of the lungs; fatal.

A nurse brings him some pills and when she leaves he throws them under the bed. 'I'm not afraid of death,' he tells me, 'but I will not become a vegetable!'

They send him home to die, but I know he'll get better. 'If I can only eat,' he says. 'If I can gain some weight.' Little beads of perspiration form on his upper lip as he tries to eat. It's such an effort. He gets thinner and thinner. His back takes on a strange twisted painful shape, but I'm still sure he'll get better. My father can't die. I want him to go to the movies and see his daughter on the screen and be proud of me.

Alan Pakula has asked me to do a little part in his film *Klute*. On the set I look for Jane Fonda. I've seen her in *Barbarella* and expect a statuesque blonde sex symbol. It takes me by surprise to be introduced to a rather small brown-haired woman with ink on her hands, but when we do a scene together I can see how intense she is, how fascinating.

My parents give a bitter-sweet thirtieth wedding anniversary party. All their friends come and have drinks and a lobster dinner around the pool as they have done together for so many years. When the guests have gone my father and I sit out on the terrace and talk about life and death. 'I don't mind,' he says. 'I've been very happy, done everything I ever dreamed of. If I lived longer, it would only be a repeat.' 'Daddy, don't you believe in God, in a life after death?' 'No,' he answers, 'I don't. When you're dead, you're dead.'

And too soon my mother and I have to drive in the black limousine to the cemetery, through rows of tombstones opening like doors into the next world.

After the funeral I go back to London and find my husband living with another woman. They want me to leave. 'It's better if you leave and we keep Jean-Paul,' they tell me. 'After all you're working and travelling and we have a nice house with a garden for Jean-Paul and his school is nearby. We're more of a family and Evie is a wonderful cook,' volunteers Marc. My father has been dead a week. Dazed, I agree, but I see Jean-Paul every spare minute I have. We spend every weekend together going to museums, films, the park. We sleep in my bed together and talk about everything. 'Daddy doesn't love me,' he says one evening as we snuggle up together. 'Why do you say that?' I ask. 'He never takes me to movies and things like you do.' Every time I drop him off he cries and I feel torn apart. 'You do that on purpose, making a big scene,' Marc accuses. I ignore this and take him aside and give him £10. 'Take Jean-Paul to the movies, or the zoo or something.' The next weekend Jean-Paul is full of stories about a trip to the zoo, and the animals he saw and lunch in the park.

At Christmas I sit in my room with its little tree smoking endless cigarettes. 'In the New Year,' I think, 'I will begin again.'

CHAPTER 4

'Come over and have lunch with me, I'm at the Milan Grand,' Gunilla says.

I've been lying in bed all morning smoking, too depressed to get up. 'I'm not hungry.'

'They're making a movie here with Pierre Clementi,' she tempts me, knowing he's my favourite actor.

So we sit in the lobby after lunch and watch them filming *Una Vittima Designata* with Tomas Milian and Pierre.

'I'd love to be in this film,' I say dreamily.

'Don't be ridiculous,' she says.

A balding Italian who has been staring since we arrived comes over. '*Permesso* – you are a mosta beautiful woman I ever see,' he says to me. 'Please, I wanna you be ina my film.'

I give Gunilla a little cat smile and two days later I arrive in Venice to play Pierre's girlfriend.

Venice isn't a city. It is a dream floating on the sea. In

the hotel the director takes me to Pierre's for a script conference. His room, darkened by squares of silk hung over lamps, smells of incense, an atmosphere of decadence and church. The table a jumble of personal pictures, Madonnas, crucifixes, loose tobacco and letters.

Pierre is lying in bed surrounded by books and notebooks. Beautiful, pale as marble. The holy guardian angel is smoking hashish. He takes the joint out of his mouth and puts it between my lips. There are no words. I sit on the end of the bed; the chairs are covered with clothes, while the director walks up and down talking. 'Youra relationship,' he explains. 'She is *misteriosa*. The people no understand.' I feel Pierre watching me, feel a current vibrating between us, but I don't dare to look at him. We decide to go downstairs to dinner. Pierre throws back the covers and gets out of bed. He is stark naked. If he wants to shock me he has succeeded.

Perfume's sweetness is released only when it evaporates, just as Pierre's radiance can't be contained, can barely be captured on film. Experimental, a favourite of artists like Bunuel and Pasolini. He is the Steppenwolf.

He coaches me for my role before the camera and off; on the canals, and cafes, the restaurant where he hardly eats. He dares everything: drugs, the passion, art, and the Holy Roman Church. The mystic outlaw lover. Fascinated, I follow where he leads, pushing past all and any limits, distractions into another sphere, a sphere of unnameable longing. Like Orpheus I follow him down into the underworld, where he is as doomed as Eurydice. He tells me, 'You are the Madonna, my Madonna; I worship only you.' He gets down on his knees. 'Don't,' I say.

Before the year is out, they will send him to prison for drugs. I leave him in Venice, the train travelling along the sea, over the land and away, and as it runs it sings *my song*, 'I am the ice queen, so proud and free, I thought that just one sweet kiss could never touch me.' Louder and louder, faster and faster it runs and the metal wheels singing *my song*. 'I've lost my peace, my body's way ahead of thinking, I'm in the sea and sinking.' It rushes by Verona, home of Romeo and Juliet, 'In your arms am I dreaming, drugged, alive and more aware. This is all I want of heaven and earth. Hold me here.'

Yes, hold me. To sleep alone terrifies me, to be forever alone is unbearable, so I am never alone. There is the amorous sheik who offers me everything and anything if only I would . . . if only I will. I'm not interested in his gifts, his jewellery, his yacht or him. It drives him crazy. At Annabel's he spends £100 on a bottle of wine to impress me. A great fuss is made. The year, the rarity, as the bottle is brought in by a waiter who practically scrapes the ground in deference. 'Your Highness, the wine.' A reverential hush falls over the table as with great ceremony the waiter pours a little of the wine into a glass. Ahmed sniffs. 'Ah, the bouquet.' He sips, he swirls the wine around his tongue savouring it. The knowing look, 'Ah, yes.'

Back at his Mayfair house, drunk on his £100 wine, he pins me to the sofa. He won't take no for an answer this time. 'All right, all right, just let me go to the bathroom first.' I smile seductively while straightening my clothes, leaving him lolling on the sofa in his caftan. In the bathroom I run the water in the sink, open the window, climb out and hightail it home.

There is Pat DeCicco, 'the turnip king', ex-husband of Gloria Vanderbilt who follows me to Milan and teaches me about guns. Ronan O'Reilly, who started Radio Caroline, the first radio pirate station talks to me about 'loving awareness'. There are assorted playboys and minor princes. By now, there is a lot of drinking of Southern Comfort.

A famous movie producer, a heavy-set Hungarian in his sixties takes me to dinner at the White Elephant to meet Cubby Broccoli, producer of the James Bond pictures, and we spend a pleasant enough evening.

Driving home with the Hungarian through the rainy London streets, I look out of the window at the street lamps along the Mall reflected in the wet road. I'm deep in thought when hearing heavy breathing I turn to see him staring at me, his hand in his trousers on his juddering sex; I see the sweat on his jowly face hanging like lice on the beetroot skin. 'Oh, God!' I recoil in horror. 'I'm an old man,' he rasps. 'I only want to look,' he begs. My dinner comes up in my throat. I feel sick and ashamed and fearful that I have somehow caused this scene.

Arriving at my house I jump out of the car before the chauffeur can open the door. I'm sick in the bushes halfway down the walk. The next night I stay home alone, high on morphine.

A film director gives me the use of his white Rolls-Royce whenever I like. The chauffeur lets slip that he is married. I'm furious! At the Henry Cooper fight we have our own terrific fight. I tell him exactly what I think of him. 'If you were a man I'd slap your face,' he snarls, and 'If you were a man,' I say, 'I'd slap yours!'

I have five boyfriends all called Peter. Two dozen yellow roses arrive, with a card, 'Love, Peter'.

I try to fill my empty restlessness with books. *Sidhartha, Be Here Now*, Carlos Castenada, the Tibetan *Book of the Dead*; Torah, tantra, yantra, mantra; going to the Buddhist Centre; to church. I join a study group at the home of the local vicar looking for inspiration, for answers; I am haunted by God. I need to know what is true, what is right, what God wants. The vicar tells me, 'Follow your conscience.' Annoyed, I wonder if Christ will keep dying till death is dead.

Still looking for answers I take an LSD trip. Storming heaven's gates, exalted inviting of madness. I'm as nervous as I am before flying, not even sure I can do it, but I swallow a sliver of transparent 'window pane' and wait. Twenty minutes pass, nothing. I look down at the carpet and suddenly the lines move. I look closer. The patterns wiggle.

Peter Biziou, who will later win the Oscar for filming *Mississippi Burning*, and I go to Hampstead Heath. As we walk down the street I feel myself leave my body. 'I'm out, free!' I think. Below me I see Peter walking a big doll that looks like me. My shoes make me laugh. 'You think you have me, but you don't have me, not me,' I tell him.

In the park I sit alone on a hill under a large oak tree, whose myriad leaves flooded with air tinkle harshly. The ground is sparkling. A German shepherd dog runs by, stops, as if called and stands looking at me. Our eyes lock and I'm sucked into his gaze, completely forgetting myself. He drops his ball and comes and lies down beside me. A squirrel approaches. Bit by bit, closer and closer he comes. He's dressed in a little grey fur coat. Yes, that's what it is, a little coat and I'm wearing a coat, too, a coating really, and the dog who rests his head on my lap: he's dressed like a dog!

In the evening, Peter and I take a bath together. I've decided never to speak again. I know instinctively that I can stay high if I don't get involved with words. We sit looking at each other. The bath is lit by candles. 'What was going on with those animals?' he asks. Silence. 'You're not speaking,' he says. I look into his green eyes, sea eyes, that I love. 'Can you speak?' I smile. 'You don't want to speak.' I rest my head on his shoulder. He puts his arms around me. The water is warm. He's worried about me. I have to speak for his ease. 'Yes,' I say and I come down.

* * * *

I am known as a *femme fatale*. The reality is I'm a *femme fatality* – witchery, bitchery, lux whorey, buggery woe man.

In 1970 I try a little suicide . . .

Standing at the sink in the locked-door bathroom, the water running over my bare white wrist, which swims like a little fish under the faucet, belly up and vulnerable, slicing away at a thin red line which appears over the vein.

My whole being resists me and I am unable to force the cutting blade deep enough for death. I try swallowing a coward's handful of pills which makes me gag up all the hidden tears, fears; the dry sobbing desolations.

Then I take my birth-control pill, out of habit as I do

every night, and climbing into bed, wearing my prettiest nightgown, I lie down on white sheets to die.

But death is uninterested in my dramas and I wake up the next morning strangely refreshed and ready to try again – dying to live.

Suze and I drive to Paris to do the collections in her beat-up old car. A warm and funny tomboy Marilyn Monroe, she wants to quit modelling and become a photographer so she takes pictures of me all the way to France. Her boyfriend encourages her to sleep with as many men as she can believing that it will free her from her inhibitions. She thinks he's brilliant, this philosopher.

In Paris I'm immediately booked by Ungaro to do his collection. Dark, handsome and intelligent with the air of a physician, I'm surprised he's booked me because he usually likes big, sporty blonde types. I hope he isn't planning to 'redo' me.

The cherished dresses of couture, dinosaurs in exquisite materials, Alençon lace, frothy organdies, jewel-encrusted silks, and sables. There are only about three thousand women in the world who will pay upwards of $35,000 for such an outfit. In his doctor's smock Ungaro spends hours fitting me till everything is perfect, or I faint, whichever comes first.

Between fittings the models sit in the cabine at long tables cluttered with make-up before acres of mirrors, reading, knitting, smoking. 'What's that?' I ask Marianne. Her violet powder intrigues me.

'Try it.'

My skin pales and becomes luminous.

'Have it. It doesn't suit me,' she offers.

'Really?'

We all go out to lunch together at Chez Francis. Naturally thin, we eat like horses. It's a myth that models starve themselves. A bottle of champagne is sent over from Monsieur le Comte. We wave and smile appreciatively.

In the afternoon, the hairdresser arrives, which I dread. Everyone is to have their hair cut in a Dutch bob this season, he decrees. 'Oh, no!' I resist. 'I hate short hair. It's not me,' I wail. He couldn't care less. Temperamental bitch, he is probably thinking. 'Perhaps a wig, then,' he relents. The wig is fitted on my head. *'Oui, très chic,'* he clucks. I hate it. I watch my face grow red in the mirror. I go upstairs to see Ungaro feeling like Moe in the Three Stooges. *'Monsieur, c'est terrible!'* He is kind. He smiles at my distress. 'No, it's not you,' he agrees. 'I'll design something special for you.'

At the opening of the collection, the excitement is palpable backstage. Dressers run around between rails of clothes checking the order. The girls are putting on their make-up, teasing their hair. Undressed and less; their slim, strict bodies, drenched in chemical flowers, lean into the mirrors to adjust an eyelash. The hairdresser pulls my hair as he rolls it up on curling tongs making me smudge my lipstick. 'Damn!,' I say under my breath.

Outside in the salon, the crowd is arriving, the press, fashion editors and arbiters, film stars Catherine Deneuve and Anouk Aimee, jet-set society ladies, sumptuous bottoms stringently dieted to fit the little gold chairs. Many are wearing their Ungaro's from the last collection, like a badge of membership in an elite club.

Pushed and pulled along an assembly line, I'm flung into the immaculate clothes, jewels clipped on to my ears; Ungaro himself adjusts a bow.

As I step out into a wall of light, cameras flash and click approval. I dance down the runway to the beat of music and applause. A Brazilian blonde in the front row takes down numbers in a crocodile-skin notebook.

The collection is a success. Ungaro comes modestly down the runway. The cabine fills with congratulation.

Afterwards, there is the rush to get away, to walk down anonymous streets in jeans and comfortable shoes carrying the pink azalea plant Ungaro gives me as a gift.

Waiting to do a screen test for Jean Aurel, I hang around Paris with Phoenix, the daughter of the head of the Greek Orthodox Church, and a group of friends on their way to Morocco. I live in an empty apartment full of parquet and French doors, empty walls painted with slogans, eating opium and experimenting with heroin, needing ten high years.

I'm sitting in my room, feeling the weight of an afternoon filled with promise, when a beautiful boy enters. Delicate, almost feminine, with hair to his waist, he comes in quietly and sits down on the floor in front of me. His beauty is startling, but he's friendly, an American, named Wahundra, and talkative. I listen, but not to the words. I hear something under and around the words.

There is a presence almost of another person. Emotion? Attraction? Love? To break the tension I ask him if he feels it, too. 'Oh, that's Krishna,' he says. 'What's

Krishna?' I ask. 'God', is his answer.

'Listen to this,' he says as he puts a record on the player. 'Bhajan from India. Songs glorifying God.'

As the first clean notes soar upward, I hear the transformation of God into sound. It is this experience which inspired men to labour for hundreds of years to build a cathedral they will never see. In this must lie the secret of the smiles of the martyrs at death. It speaks of God, to God, is God. Radiant as a blade it pierces to the core of my heart, shudders my body with pleasure, inflicting a precise killing wound.

'Who's singing?' I ask. 'Jamuna. She's a disciple of my spiritual master, Srila Prabhupada.'

We lie on the floor in front of the fire listening to the record over and over and over and over. We tell each other everything: life stories, loves and drugs; his love of boys and mine. He decides to reform me. He teaches me about Vedanta, spiritual knowledge and Lord Chaitanya, an incarnation of God as the perfect devotee, who appeared in Bengal five hundred years ago.

I leave the house three days later, slightly surprised to find Paris is still going on, to have dinner with Suze at La Coupoule. She has met the editor of *Screw* magazine and gone to an orgy. She dined with a famous writer and his model girlfriend and the girl had seduced her. 'She was so giving, she didn't want anything.' I tell her all about Wahundra and we compare adventures, eat *escargots* and drink absinthe from the nickel-plated bar.

But I don't have time to think too deeply as I have to hurry to Barcelona to do the ads for Mygurgia perfume. Soon after every time I turn a corner or go into an apothecaria, I see a poster of myself looking back at me.

Jean-Paul comes out to join me and we ride around the city in a horse-drawn carriage, walk down the Ramblas where we want to let all the birds out of their cages and eat paella washed down with Sangria, which I mistakenly think is fruit punch.

We take a boat to Ibiza for a holiday between the town and the sea. Ibiza Town is a wonderful theatre of rich hippies. We both love to people-watch. We sit in the café and see a blonde Valkyrie in a black leather bikini and boots dismount from a Harley Davidson and saunter down the street. A girl in white lace runs by crying. A man runs after her. In the sea, beautiful women bathe naked with ropes of turquoise around their necks and heavily kohled eyes.

Jean-Paul and I go to the beach in the morning. It's heaven to bake in the sun and play in the warm water together. Lunching in our wet bathing suits with salt water trickling down our backs, eating fresh salads and chewy bread, he listens with great kindness to my problems. He's doing a great job of bringing me up. He hates my smoking. Since my father's death of lung cancer, I chain smoke menthol and, in Spain, black tobacco. 'This is the last one,' I promise, but I'm too nervous to stop.

I tell him about Wahundra and we experiment with training our minds to focus intensely on the moment; and realize how half-lived life usually is. In the whitewashed siestas, I teach him a meditation. Concentrating on our breathing, we lie on our beds and feel our stomachs going up and down under our sun-burned skin, which makes us burst into laughter.

We take a trip to Formentara to visit some friends. When Jean-Paul makes friends with the local children and goes off to play on the seaweed beach, in a grove of olive trees, I meet a gypsy who offers to read the cards for me. 'Is it expensive?' I ask. 'There is no charge for you.' A storm is pushing up so we go into a cave. 'Shuffle the deck,' he says, 'and concentrate.' He lays out the cards. The hangman. 'No, shuffle again. You didn't do it thoroughly enough.' I shuffle again and again he lays out the cards. The hangman! 'Does this mean I'm going to die?' 'Not necessarily, but something will die. Some change is coming.'

The vacation ends too quickly. Jean-Paul must go back to school and I have to go to Puerto Rico to do a cigarette commercial and then on to Mexico for Aeronaves Airways. I get to spend a little time with my mother at our place in Puerto Rico as my life is running faster and faster away from me.

In my mother's flat in Puerto Rico, lying in bed, my body moist and warm from my bath, lulled by the heat, clean sheets; the air conditioner's crooning tune. In that narcotic time just before sleep, suspended between the day and the dream, my mind drifts slowly, seeking easy pleasures in lazy reverie. I let images float up on flood waters awash with bits of daily life; with lovers, fresh mangoes; with jewels and heroes; seduction and St Francis. I drop ideas into this twilight pool, mislay them, lose them and dredge them up again. Slowly I turn on the surface of my daytime mind, slowly turn and dive and drift and am sucked down into sleep.

Going behind my eyes now, I sense fear scuffling in the humid darkness; against the hard resistance of unnamed guilt, anxiety eats away until the darkness turns inside out, squeezes and drops, like a repugnant fertile egg, the knowledge of some bestial crime denied and buried under the dark seas of the unconscious. Then floating slowly towards me, borne upwards on the current of human grief, rising like a riddle, there appears under the transparent skin of a wave, the shocking white face of my child; thin-boned, hungry and alone, he stretches out his little hand, a mute paw, so fragile in its hope and so unknowing – my child, my soul.

In the next room the phone rings catapulting me violently out of sleep and jangling my nerves. My heart like a heavy iron machine shudders convulsively against my body, as I lie trembling in sheets all twisted and struggled.

I go slowly into the bathroom saying like an ancient mantra 'only a dream, only a dream'.

On the terrace my mother dressed in a bright caftan is having her coffee. The morning shocks my eyes making my head and neck ache sharply.

'Good morning, my darling,' she says cheerily, 'Would you like some breakfast? I've bought you some delicious strawberries.'

I look at the fruit moistly leaking bloody juices in its plate and feeling slightly nauseous, I sit down. 'You know I never eat breakfast,' I tell her.

'How's about some nice eggs then,' she continues, ignoring me.

'Just some juice,' I say.

'Or some toast,' she goes on. 'I have some delicious cherry preserves.'

'No,' I resist, 'just . . .'

'Well, I can make you a nice hot bowl of oatmeal with butter and sugar.'

I ease my words through clenched teeth trying not to show any irritation. 'No, just juice, thanks.'

'Well, please yourself,' she says tightly.

I pick up my glass and feel a sudden urge to throw it against the wall, to hurl it full force on to the concrete seven storeys below. The word 'SMASH' like a sign pops into my mind. I look at the word; ignore it, and drink my juice.

'How did you sleep?' she asks.

'Fine,' I say, sullen as the electric chair.

My mother lights a cigarette. 'Now,' she begins again, 'what are you wearing to the casino tonight? I want you to look especially beautiful when you go out with me.'

'Oh, I don't know,' I say evasively, 'perhaps the red satin.'

I get up and look over the balcony. The weight of seven floors pulls me forward, gravity sucking at my feet. 'JUMP' the sign flashes.

'I'm having lunch with Greta Garbo,' she says, 'I'm going to the beach,' I say,

'Be careful. Don't drown,' she laughs.

At 8 pm sharp, we're standing in the hall waiting for the elevator, a little stiff, the way women are at the start of an evening in formal clothes.

The elevator door opens and I hesitate before stepping in. Under my feet I picture the bottomless dark shaft, the heavy cables coiling and uncoiling. I imagine the newspaper report: 'plunged to their death, faulty cable snaps.' I hold my breath and to reassure myself, look at the floor numbers as they light up. The elevator stops and a couple gets in. 'Oh, how beautiful' gasps the lady looking at me through glasses edged with rhines-

Alchemy: the art of changing base metal into gold.

My maternal grandparents: 'minor aristocrats of blood and iron'.

My parents – 'a month after they were married, she fell in love with him'.

Mother and me – 'my mother was my world'.

2 years –
'before memory'.

'A perfect illusion
trapped in mirrors
full of cameras'.

'I enamel my lips with the juice of rubies'.

Marc Morrel – 'Borders which never
existed are crossed'.

With Jean-Paul – 'He's doing a
good job of bringing me up'.

Poster for my exhibition – 'So many pictures inside my head, they're flowing
out of my eyes'.

tones. 'I just know I've seen you before. Haven't I seen her in *Vogue*, honey?' She turns to a watery little man in a plaid sports coat for confirmation and gets none.

'My daughter is one of the top models in Europe,' my mother says conspiratorially.

I read the sign: 'Should not exceed 2,000 lb capacity.'

The woman peers intently into my face, her face so close I can see the road map of wrinkles etched in the thick blue eyeshadow. 'Are those your own eyelashes?' she asks.

The casino, where stale-skinned women, night-jaundiced, with cold diamonds at their necks, sit in smoky triangles of light and watch while croupiers slide plastic wafers to them in unholy communion; where men negotiate deals with fortune, and turning a card, try to rearrange the numbers in their preordained files; who plot like Luddites to break the machinery of the universe.

I wander like an immigrant and listen to the talk of winning and feel the vibration, the secret sex thrill of losing. My mother sits playing out her theories, her small victories. She introduces me to a blunt-bodied man with red hair, Mr Tosi. 'Of course you remember him, darling, he used to hold you on his knee when you were six.' He invites me to go to the Dominican Republic with him, fly down in his private plane as he has some of his factories to look at. I'm not sure I can handle the plane. 'Oh, go ahead,' my mother says, 'It will do you good.'

Early the next morning, I arrive at the airfield to find Mr Tosi strutting up and down the tarmac like a small red rooster eager as the dawn. 'You're even more beautiful in daylight,' he says, taking my bag and stowing it in the back of his plane. 'Oh, wait.' I panic, eyeing the plane which looks like a small mosquito with its fragile shell and single propeller. 'I need my valium. I can't fly . . . fly without it.' 'Nonsense,' he says confidently hustling me into the cockpit. 'You won't need that with me.'

The delicate plane trembles down the runway, lifts lightly and the ground slowly pulls away. As the earth recedes, I feel dizzy, sick with anxiety and my mind's concentration blurs as I lose my equilibrium. I feel like I'm falling backwards and strain forwards, my head almost on my knees, my seat belt tightening across my stomach like a tourniquet. I listen intently, waiting for the sputter, waiting for the engine to die and the plane to hang for a long moment before it drops in one long scream into the sea. My mind runs another nightmare newsreel: 'Lost off the coast of Puerto Rico: at 8.50 am observers saw a fireball engulf . . .'

We bank sharply to the right and I shift violently to the left trying to balance the plane and keep it from tipping over. 'Don't be nervous,' he says with a paternal chuckle. His meaty hand, covered in large brown liver spots, reaches out and pats mine and stays.

We land in a sultry heat-heavy paradise. The resort, a millionaires' club, lies on a refreshingly iced blue-green sea, fringed with sun-varnished palms. It also lies crushingly on the back and body of harsh brown-skinned poverty. We pass a pale blue lozenge of a swimming pool where bathers are being served exotic drinks decorated with chunks of mango harpooned on small paper umbrellas by native boys in white gloves. We are escorted to our rooms down a breezeway hung with baskets of fragrant flowers. We pass maids carrying stacks of fresh linens; young girls who work for mean men's wages, for money that gives no chance and no change.

Earlier on the road, I'd seen the shacks, the peeling Coca-Cola signs, the empty hunger in curious eyes as the limousine glided past the gates, past the unemployed farmers, the landless, the men of no voice and no power, men of wrong colour, workers in the factories of Mr Tosi.

'Which is my room?' I ask.

'You can stay in my room,' he answers.

'Oh, no,' I say, 'No, really. Which is my room? I've got a terrific headache. I really need to rest a little.'

'You can rest here. Why don't we just lie down on my bed and take a nap together?' he says.

'No,' I say.

'Well, you lie down. I want to see what you look like lying down.'

'I look the same, up or down,' I say, trying to keep things light.

He eyes me cynically. 'C'mon, you're a big girl and I'm a big boy.'

'But, you're married!' I sputter. 'Your wife's a friend of my mother. You knew my father.'

'Don't be so naive,' he says. 'I'm sure your father had his fun, too; all men do!'

'Not my father!' My headache is unbearable. He glances at his watch.

'Look, I have to go to the factory and take care of some business. Here's your key. You rest, have a swim. I'll pick you up for dinner at eight.'

My room is lovely and cool with a sunken tub, fresh

fruit in a basket and a little mint on the pillow. Outside is a private garden for sunbathing. The maid comes in with a vase of orchids and a note saying, 'See you at eight.'

I don't know why, but I feel like crying all the time lately. I can't sleep and I refuse to cry about nothing, so I smoke till it's time to get ready for dinner.

I take a bath and begin to get dressed but as I put on my make-up, I start to sweat. The room is cool from the air conditioning, but I'm sweating so much my make-up keeps running, so I take another bath to calm myself and start again. I look at the clock anxiously. It's getting late. The sweat keeps prickling up through the make-up. I have another cigarette to calm down. I'm afraid of being late. I powder frantically. I try to put on my lipstick, but my hand is shaking so badly that I have to hold the brush with both hands. I keep powdering the sweat and smoking and by eight I'm ready and almost blind with a headache.

Dinner is by the pool. Exotic flowers decorate a huge buffet of giant lobster, mounds of shrimp on crushed ice and tubs of caviar. A Mariachi band feverishly plays sambas. 'Let's dance,' he orders, pulling me on to the dance floor where he presses his bulky body against me, running his hands up and down me possessively. I recoil. He pulls me closer. 'Relax, let yourself go.' His breath in my face is rancid. Revolted, I pull away.

'I'm sorry I'm being such a bore,' I apologize. 'I don't feel well. My head is so bad. I've got to leave.'

'Shall I come in and give you a massage?' he leers.

'No . . . No, thank you. Thank you, no.'

By the time I return from the trip, I am in constant

pain but the doctor my mother takes me to tells me, after finishing his examination, that there is nothing wrong with me physically. 'Well, why do I have this pain in my head?'

'Aside from the pain, how do you feel?' he asks.

'Frightened.'

'Of what?'

'Of everything. It's too silly.'

'Have you had a shock, a lot of stress in your life?'

'Yes, who doesn't.'

'You need rest,' he advises. 'You're on the verge of a nervous breakdown. It's not serious, but you should see a therapist, someone you can talk to; and rest.'

Good advice to be ignored.

* * * *

Marc has broken up with his girlfriend and gone to live in Amsterdam, so Jean-Paul and I live together now in the house on Addison Road. He is anxious to go to the temple in Bury Place that Wahundra talked about and to meet Mukunda.

Mukunda turns out to be a young monk from America; a gentle humorous person with great warmth. He invites us to take *prasadam*. *Prasadam*, he explains, is food offered to God. It's a Sanskrit word meaning the mercy of God and that they are vegetarians because Krishna only accepts vegetarian food and besides why cause pain unnecessarily when you can eat very nicely, more economically and more healthily without it. The *prasadam* is wonderful, the best food I have ever eaten. While we eat, sitting cross-legged on the floor, Mukunda explains that Krishna is a Sanskrit word meaning 'all attractive' and is a name of God; he says that there is one God, but that He has unlimited names. Jean-Paul is fascinated by the deities. 'The spiritual master is coming next week. Why don't you come and meet him?' Mukunda asks.

CHAPTER 5

The day that Srila Prabhupada is arriving, the whole temple is in a frenzy of activity. Flower garlands are being made, and special *prasadam* prepared; the temple cleaned and decorated. As the hour draws near, the devotees gather outside for a rousing *kirtan.* * *Hare* Krishna, *Hare* Krishna, Krishna, Krishna, *Hare Hare*, *Hare* Rama, *Hare* Rama, Rama, Rama, *Hare, Hare,* fills the air! Shaven-headed monks with white clay on their foreheads in Indian robes, girls in saris holding flower garlands, devotees, their faces shining with enthusiasm and purity, leap and dance on the sidewalk in front of the temple. The crash of the *kartals* and beat of the drums reverberates the maha mantra† down the quiet London street, as they chant. In the neighbouring house a curtain is pulled aside and disapproving faces appear at the window.

* Devotional music used in saying the name, or praising the Lord.
† The great mantra of deliverance.

Because we are guests, Jean-Paul and I are placed at the front of all this leaping, dancing and chanting where we stand mute, glued to the ground in embarassment. 'I'm certainly not going to bow down to him!' I say and Jean-Paul agrees.

The car pulls up and as the door opens, the chanting rises to a roar. The first thing I see is a little foot, sweet as a child's and then Srila Prabhupada emerges. Inexplicably both Jean-Paul and I burst into tears and throw ourselves on to the ground in front of him to pay our obeisances with the devotees.

He strolls majestically into the temple, chin jutting out, eyes like laser beams. We crowd in after him, see him pay his obeisance to the deities and take his seat on the *vyasasan*.* The small temple room is packed and in the crush I lose Jean-Paul. Scanning the room for him, I finally find him sitting at Srila Prabhupada's feet. Srila Prabhupada sits looking down at him. He asks Mukunda, 'Who is this little boy?'

Mukunda tells him, 'He is Jean-Paul.'

'No! He is not,' says Srila Prabhupada, 'He is St John.'

The room is hushed expectantly as he takes up his *kartals* and slowly begins to sing the haunting '*Jaya Radha Madhava.*' When he finishes he closes his eyes. He seems to be listening. 'So,' he begins, 'We are not the body but eternal spirit souls.' He explains Bhakti Yoga†, the science of self-realization and how to attain

---

* Honoured seat of the spiritual master, who is considered a representative of Vyas, reputed author of the Vedas.
† Selfless spiritual devotion and service as the means of linking up to the Supreme.

love of God through the purifying chanting of God's holy names: *japa mala*. He speaks simply and once tears fill his eyes and his voice breaks. 'The Lord is so kind,' he says and falls silent.

Here is a man who has given his life to God; as he tells one disciple, 'there never was a time when I forgot Krishna.' The world's outstanding Sanskrit scholar, he is translating the Vedic scriptures, the spiritual knowledge of the East into English. He has left the peace of the Radha Damodar temple in Vrndavan and come to America at seventy, ill with a heart condition, with only $7 in his pocket following the order of his spiritual master and Lord Chaitanya to preach the message of God in every town and village. He is so charismatic, his message so potent, the teaching so powerful, that a young disciple asks him, 'Are you God?' In a fury Srila Prabhupada slams his fist on the table, 'No!' he explodes, 'I am the servant of the servant of the servants of God. Many times removed.'

Jean-Paul falls in love with Srila Prabhupada; with the temple and the devotees. He makes little Jaganath* Deities out of toilet-paper rolls and sets up an altar in his bedroom, lighting incense and saying the prayers he learns from the devotees. Mukunda becomes Uncle Mukunda and Jean-Paul often spends the weekends at the temple with him. The night after Srila Prabhupada's arrival we are having dinner at home. I've prepared Jean-Paul's favourite meal: lamb chops, peas, mashed potatoes and mint jelly. 'Mommy, I don't want to eat a lamb,' he says. The realization that the chop on the plate

* A special deity of Lord Krishna as Lord of the Universe.

is the remnants of a lamb and the suffering it must have endured to get there, unnecessary suffering, strikes home; we become vegetarians.

One afternoon, I come home late to find Jean-Paul, scissors in hand, cutting off his beautiful golden curls. 'Jean-Paul!' Violet-blue eyes gaze at me. I am about to lecture him angrily but he looks so sad and so funny with tufts of hair sticking out all over his head and little bald spots – the mouse who got caught in the lawnmower – I can't help but laugh. 'Jean-Paul, what am I going to do with you?'

'Can I shave my head like the devotees?' he asks.

'Might as well,' I say, 'It couldn't look any worse.

Jean-Paul longs to be a devotee. He wants formal initiation and a spiritual name. With great courage he comes before the spiritual master, Srila Prabhupada, who offers him a *sandesh*, an Indian milk sweet instead. 'No, thank you,' he says politely. He is determined to have a name. The initiation, the acceptance of the spiritual master has already taken place in his heart. The Sanyasis[*] wait to see what will happen. After a long pause, Srila Prabhupada says, 'Your name is Annimisha Das. Annimisha means one who doesn't blink and therefore can always see Krishna.' Completely satisfied, Annimisha accepts his *sandesh*.

Sitting in front of the deities, I am thinking about what Srila Prabhupada had said to me in his room earlier. 'Now you are cold, but if you just stand in the sun for a while, you will become warm. Chanting is like that. Just try it and you will get warm, when he comes

* One who has taken Sanyasa. Sanyasa is the fourth and last of the ashrams – spiritual divisions of the human life cycle – renunciate or monk.

into the temple room surrounded by his senior disciples.' I turn and pay my obeisance to him, but being ignorant I put my feet towards the deities. 'No, no,' he says, 'like this.' Then paying his obeisances, he shows me the correct way. I stand, looking down at the tiny figure. 'So,' he beckons, 'you do it.' I pay my obeisance as he has done. We lie side by side on the marble floor. His brown eyes twinkle into mine. 'Do you understand?' he asks, 'Yes, Srila Prabhupada,' I lie.

* * * *

'Don't be afraid,' says Tom, an old friend from Munich. It reminds me of the last time I had seen Srila Prabhupada, when he had pointed his finger at me and said, 'I can make you fearless,' but Prabhupada leaves for India and Jean-Paul goes off to boarding school.

To be alone is a disease, an infectious yellow fear. In nights made of iron, I am forced through a door whose inscription I can't read.

'I'm having a nervous breakdown,' I tell Tom. I haven't actually thought about it since I left Puerto Rico.

'I'll take care of you,' he says, 'Don't you know I've always been in love with you? We'll go to Italy, where it's warm.'

I begin to cry.

'Tell me what's wrong,' he says.

My mind wraps around a dark bundle filled with dread. I'm ashamed. I can't unwrap it in front of him, let him see it all fall out on my clean white face, stuff in my mouth, my eyes bloody with excess. I cry harder, my sobs like stones bruising my chest, I haven't the courage.

I try to push it all back but it keeps dripping through the cracks in my mind. I can't stop crying.

He takes me in his arms, 'Yes cry, it's good for you. Let it all out.' He slowly undresses me, soothing me and gently begins to make love to me. All my resistance is washed away by my tears, I cling to him. 'Do you want it?'

'Yes, oh yes.' To be in love always solves my problems.

The flowers are on fire . . . electric light is dripping on the floor . . . Sitting here with Tom in the psychiatrist's office with its obvious fish tank and crazy people. Am I mad, too? The pressure of sanity is exhausting me. I remember my friend Sherri, who had gone mad and seen blood coming out of her shower.

'Am I crazy?' I blurt out to the psychiatrist who smiles and says, 'Not at all. It's just stress. Take these pills. See me next month.' But I don't see him next month. The pills give me the shakes and Tom makes me throw them away and takes me to live in Italy.

* * * *

His Holiness, the Pope, spends his summers in Castel Gandolfo, a small town on a volcanic lake overlooking Rome where Tom and I take a large villa complete with gardener and Alsatian guard dog. The terracotta floors remain cool under our bare feet, the windows open out on to the lake and soft breezes; from the terrace, ringed with earthenware pots filled with pink and orange geraniums, Rome glimmers in the distance. In our garden a huge fig tree blossoms and the fruit, hot-seeded and ripe, makes a feast for the birds and overflows into the house in jams and jellies. And we love each other, our bodies sun warm, salted from trips to the sea, hungry.

The table fork, unknown in Europe before the Renaissance, was first used in Italy. We delight in the cuisine of Italy, in dishes of *penne arrabiata*, a fat spicy pasta, or *fettucini al burro*, ribbon noodles cooked in butter and cheese. We drive in the hilly countryside, listening to Stevie Wonder and Dr John, sit in trattorias under grape vines drinking the bitter Verdicchio Dei Castelli di Jesi from the Marches of Central Italy, straw-coloured Frascati, the flinty red Barbaresco from Turin, sit in complicated silence, looking down at the lake, said to be so deep that when an airplane crashed in it and sank, it could not be recovered.

After a siesta, swollen with heat, we walk among the dead of ancient Rome, who grow in the weeds of the Forum. A pale blue wild flower, part-Christian martyr, part-gladiator, nestles among the fallen columns of the Coliseum. Weeds whisper on the Appia Antica and piles of silent skulls swim among the fish of the Catacombs.

Late at night we stop in a café near the Spanish Steps and drink Sambucca *con la mosca* – Sambucca with a fly – the fly being a coffee bean, which we crush between our teeth as we sip. Our kisses are sweet and sticky, aniseed-flavoured caresses all the way up the mountain.

In the summer, the big house becomes hospitable. Claudia and Wolfgang, friends from Munich, come to visit and shop. Aixa Aiosa, a girlfriend from America with a rambunctious baby, appears. My mother arrives and gives us advice on furnishing the villa and takes us to a dressed-up dinner on the roof of the Hassler and later Tom's brother, the actor Ian Nicholas, spends the summer and digs a vegetable garden for us. We make friends with the composer Hans Werner Henze and are often invited for dinner and a game of *bocci* at his beautiful villa nearby.

Jean-Paul arrives for his holidays and, in July, Ian takes us to the Festa di Noantri in the Roman quarter of Trastevere and wins him a goldfish in a plastic bag. Jean-Paul tells me about his new school, Stoke Brunswick which he loves, 'except for the food. It's terrible and there isn't enough,' he complains. We reminisce about Prabhupada and the devotees. He tells me, 'I have a devil and an angel inside my head, but don't worry, mommy,' he reassures me. 'The angel always wins.'

The summer ends, the weather changes and violent storms attack the mountain. Blinding walls of white light flash across a black sky. The eruptions of torrential rain whip a loose shutter back and forth and thunder crashes against the house breaking the electricity and terrifying me. Hiding under the bedclothes, I feel the full force of the storm inside my body.

I become sick again and again with bronchitis. The doctor comes and gives me antibiotics and tells me to stay in bed and stop smoking.

Bored with bed and being sick, Tom and I are playing gin rummy. I'm winning when I begin to feel funny. 'Go to bed,' Tom tells me. 'The doctor told you to stay in bed.'

'No!' I insist. 'Something's really wrong.' But he doesn't believe me.

I watch in horror as thick red welts pop out on my

arms and my fingers swell together into a mitt. 'Oh, my God, look, Tom they're all over my stomach!' I feel dizzy as Tom helps me to bed. Half-way there, I choke. 'I can't breathe! I can't see!'

The next thing I know, the room is full of men in white. 'What did you take?' they ask. 'Are you cold?'

'Cold!' I try to think, to remember what cold is like.

It's anaphalactic shock, an allergic reaction to the antibiotic. They give me an injection and carry me out to the waiting ambulance. I can hear the siren as we careen down the streets. In spite of feeling sicker than I ever imagined I could feel, it's all very exciting. I must admit I'm rather pleased to get a ride in an ambulance.

Tom's face is close to mine, his long blond hair brushing my cheek. 'I love you,' he whispers. I look down at my aching hands, to find my nails have turned black.

My body knows before I do, what I don't want to admit. Tom and I. It doesn't work. We are too different with too much attraction, always pulling in opposite directions. He sleeps till noon. I want to share the sunrise. He is silent. I want to talk. I believe in marriage, expect marriage. He calls it a piece of paper. He hates people staring at me and blames me for it. He is critical. I feel suffocated. I buy a motorcycle. He makes me give it back. Back and forth it goes and goes nowhere.

Tangled in desire, intoxicated by our bodies, love becomes an affliction. Unlike the great tragic lovers, saved from the threat of love by death or distance, we live too long together.

*　*　*　*

In Rome I'm noticed by a producer and asked to do a

screen test. Movies follow. I am glad to get out of the house, away from the tensions. Tom sits alone in the house on top of the mountains and sulks. 'What's wrong?' I ask.

'You know.'

'No, I don't.'

'Well, think about it.'

I don't want to think about it, can't think about it. I think instead of God.

I walk, chanting rounds, thinking and praying. Walk to the church in Castel Gandolfo. Along the road at intervals are marked the Stations of the Cross. A small candle burns illuminating a picture of the suffering Christ. A bouquet of wild flowers, pale as paper, lies wilting in the heat. 'Sweet Jesus, help me,' I pray. If I had one thing to offer, one pure and beautiful thing, a small clean thing, anything; but I have nothing.

One night after work, Tom doesn't meet me. I've spent the day working on a film with Valentina Cortese, sitting around in a freezing castle, laced into period costumes, waiting for the crew to set up the dinner-party scene. Just as the cameras are about to roll, Miss Cortese says, 'No! I can't drink this wine; it's terrible, all wrong for the scene. *Carrisimo*,' she purrs to the director, 'We must have champagne.' So we wait again till the champagne arrives and the star is happy.

We go into overtime and a snake, a sleepy-looking boa constrictor is being temperamental. 'Nice pet,' I tell the trainer. 'He's not a pet!' he says offended. 'He's a performer!'

Too proud to call Tom, I decide to walk home alone. As I leave the town a policeman stops me. '*Signorina*, it is dangerous to go alone on these roads at night. I will accompany you,' he offers. I would prefer to be alone but I say, 'How kind, *grazie*.' Half-way home, he begins to tell me how beautiful I am. '*Sposata?*' he asks. 'Married?' 'No.' He takes out his gun and begins playing with it. 'You like Italians?' 'Yes,' I say. 'You are afraid?' he asks. 'No,' I answer. Of course, I am, but I pretend I haven't seen the gun, purposely misunderstand his Italian. 'Come to my house for a drink,' I invite him. I babble on about him being a good Catholic and the Pope being down the road, how kind he is to accompany me. When we get home Tom comes out to greet us with the dog. I can see the policeman is surprised. We all have a drink together and Tom thanks him for bringing me home. After that whenever we see him in town, we wave and smile, but I never again walk on the mountain alone at night.

Tom wants to live in Munich. I dread it, but Tom insists we go. I know everything will end in Munich. Munich is a nightmare. Tom spends his days at his mother's house. We hardly speak. I'm paralyzed with the fear of losing him. No matter how much I eat, I get thinner and thinner. I wander around the stolid city, refusing to learn German.

I love him so much. I don't want us to break up, but I have to face the fact that he doesn't love me.

Lying in bed together one night, he says, 'The problem with us is that it is one-sided love.' My heart begins to pound. Now he will tell me he doesn't love me. 'The problem,' he continues, 'is that you have never loved me.'

The very next night, we have tickets for an Emerson

Lake and Palmer concert, but Tom doesn't show up. I'm walking around aimlessly, waiting, when I'm approached by an official, who tells me, 'Mr Lake has seen you and the boys in the band would like to meet you.' I follow him backstage and am introduced to the group. Everyone is very jolly. They invite me to sit on the stage with them while they play, and to dinner after the performance.

Four young gods in leather and tat strut their stuff. The audience goes wild as they belt out the music; playing the audience, teasing it, building it higher and higher; building the fire, forcing the audience to open to them, yielding to their music. Over-amped, electrified, the drum beats growing harder. The singer mouthing the microphone and the audience one body now screams and sighs in ecstasy.

In the dressing room, they are no longer gods, hardly human. One of the musicians, a towel around his neck, is having an argument over money with the promoter. Though he clearly owes the man the money, he persists in being difficult, enjoying arguing, still high on the power of the performance; playing cat with this little Kraut mouse.

Becoming bored, he looks over at me. 'Watch this,' he says and throws the money on to the floor. 'He'll pick it up,' he sneers. The man, who is old enough to be his grandfather, grovels around the floor picking up the scattered notes.

We go to their hotel, where they have kept the restaurant open especially for us. They eat like slobs, throwing bread rolls at each other, sloshing down expensive wines, calling rudely to the waiters, who show them nothing but perfect manners and courtesy. 'Yes, sir,' they say and bring anything these louts feel like ordering, satisfying their every whim. Well they will get 'no satisfaction' where I am concerned.

I come home early in the morning. Tom is in bed pretending to be asleep.

The craziness of our relationship is driving us insane. He keeps me up all night accusing me of bringing a man to our room. I try to convince him I'm innocent, have never been unfaithful, never wanted to be. 'Don't lie to me,' he shouts. 'I can see his fingerprints all over the wall!' By the morning, we're both half mad. 'I'm leaving you.' 'No!' he says. I don't want to leave him but he lets me go.

I've lost him. I can't bear to think of his eyes, his ways. Under my rib cage, the pain is constant. Sometimes he calls me in London to see how I am. 'Great,' I say cheerfully.

* * * *

Srila Prabhupada is staying at Bhaktivedanta Manor, the house George Harrison has given the devotees. I sit outside his door, chanting my rounds, happy to know he is near.

And there is always work. A French photographer books me and tells my agent, 'The client loves her look. She's so serene.' I could almost laugh if I wasn't so miserable.

Barry, a friend who has just broken up with his girlfriend, and I travel together through Europe to console ourselves. We take turns to cry on each other's shoulders. I am drunk the whole trip.

Driving through France in his old Volkswagen, we come to a crossroads and a sign pointing to Lourdes. 'C'mon, it'll be interesting.' 'Let's go,' I dare him. We drive into Lourdes in the evening and are immediately disgusted by the commercialism. Plastic statues of the Virgin, light-up scenes of the grotto, trick pictures of Christ with eyes that follow you around, a slew of guest houses, 'Religious tourism'.

We are, therefore, unprepared for the breathtaking beauty of the grotto, where 'Our Lady' appeared, and its strange afflictions. The rock ceiling is hung with crutches and canes, the refuse of miraculous cures. In row after row of wheelchairs, hope concentrates the faces of cripples. Emaciated forms are carried on stretchers into the grotto, their weak fingers making the sign of the cross into the night, as it flows, dripping with stars, rotating slowly in circles of milk.

Christ is here, waiting to interrupt the world. He is burning in the candle flames. He is on the lips, in the prayers. He is here in the sweet night air. It tastes of him, clean, curing, intoxicating.

Feeling refreshed we both give up cigarettes. This minor miracle lasts just about till we arrive back in London, where Barry introduces me to an extraordinary woman called Bunty Wills, a Jungian analyst, a white witch in the best sense of the phrase; a truly wise woman, with a wry sense of humour.

I go to her to talk about Tom, to be consoled. She asks me to keep a journal of my dreams, so I tell her the dream about my lost baby almost dying. The anguish I felt. 'Am I a bad mother?' I ask. 'No,' she explains. 'The dream is about you. The baby isn't Jean-Paul, it's your self, your soul, crying out to you because you're neglecting it.' 'Yes,' I say, anxious to get back to the subject of how I can get back together with Tom.

In my flat in Randolph Crescent I keep one large white room, with floor to ceiling windows empty, furnished only with a view of the garden. In this room I spend hours chanting the mantra Prabhupada has given me.

One evening as I'm going to a workshop downstairs from Bunty's, I accidentally meet her as she's coming down the stairs.

Without a word being said, I wake up from the everyday dream that we call life. We stand looking at each other, our gaze connected by an almost visible string of energy. I have lost myself, yet I have never been more myself. I stand at the bottom of the steps . . . in eternity.

Then she continues down the stairs, out the door and I go into the studio.

I can hardly wait for my next appointment. I'm so excited.

'What was that?' I ask, 'Did you feel it, too?'

'Of course,' she answers. She looks out of the window, her eyes silver in the bright light. A cigarette hangs from the corner of her mouth as she talks. 'That is where great saints and sages live.' The room is silent.

'I want to live there, too!' I say.

*   *   *   *

I meet Ginger Baker, probably the greatest rock drummer in the world. We become friends and he spends a lot of time at our house, entertaining us with wonderful stories of Africa, where he's built a recording studio.

Boys' Own adventure stories.

He takes us to Polo, where he rides like his music, like a wild Indian, balanced on the stirrups, his red hair flying, the stick an extension of his hand.

He stuffs Jean-Paul with candy bars and introduces me to his mother, but I can't forget Tom.

*   *   *   *

There can never be a space in my life when I'm not in love with someone; no gaps for fear to squeeze through; to feel the awful homesickness of the temporariness of things. I'm afraid I'll start screaming and not be able to stop, will scream the whole world. I don't want to face what may be ripening in the dark. I want to be a woman; ordinary, with small wishes, with kitchens and husband, family meals around a table, the sun leaning against a wall. Normal life. I want to bury myself in a man, to be safe inside him.

I meet my husband James at a dinner party I don't want to go to. I'm seated between the gorgeous Rob, a mercenary for the Sultan of Oman, and him. They both flirt outrageously, but I prefer James with his sexy bad boy face and pretty blue eyes.

He's from a fine Catholic family, who had owned old Paar Whisky and are now stockbrokers. A large family of two sisters and three brothers, growing up at Strode Manor, going to Ampleforth to be educated by the monks, who taught him not how to be good, but only to feel guilty about not being good.

He comes from county England, an England of fox hunting and gymkhanas, an England of empire, of boarding schools, with large country houses and flats in

London, a shooting, hunting, sporting society. Married to the right girl, at the right time . . . old boy's network . . . old chap. Church on Sunday, Midnight Mass at Christmas, gum boots and Burberry. 'God Save the Queen' and God save poor Jamie, who if his family hadn't been so nice, so essentially loving, would have made a perfect remittance man.

Instead they tried to fit the round peg into the square hole. Pa wants the boys in the City, in banking or brokering. Pressured, James arrives at the staid City firm of pin-striped partners on his motorbike with long hair, black cape to the ground. It isn't that he's against money. Not at all. He's just determined to do it his way.

He arrives at my house the morning after the party and never leaves. We dream of creating cheap housing for the poor, using Geodisics and the ideas of Buckminster Fuller. Jamie is full of dreams and energy. With money from his inheritance, he buys an American collector's car, a mile-long Mustang, white convertible with red leather upholstery. It lives at the garage and costs him a fortune but it makes him feel like the 'King of the Road'.

Jamie loves all things American, as only a foreigner can. He shows me a different America, a juicy roustabout, gold-rush fresh America. New York City was never America and Palm Beach . . . I've no roots, no home here, just sightseeing.

We travel across the country, stopping in New Orleans to see the muddy Mississippi, bubbling, roiling along, eat Beignets in the French Quarter and catch a glimpse of a girl in a strip club dancing on top of the bar in high-heeled shoes, a bored expression and nothing else. For the first time I understand 'the Blues'. It plays different on Beale Street.

Texas takes days to cross which gives me plenty of time to read about the American Indians. One of the books I have is full of wonderful old pictures of Indians, harsh-lit, tomahawk-sharp faces, proud as eagles.

In Arizona, we visit their reservation, driving from the hot desert floor in Phoenix where my Uncle Eddie, a former vice president of Minnesota Mining, is playing golf, up into the snow-capped mountains.

We drive for mile after flat mile with only the brilliant blue sky, the bright red earth as far as the eye can see.

On top of a *mesa*, in a village of *adobe* houses, with wooden ladders leaning against their sides, we ask to speak to the headman as we want to buy some antique jewellery, which we've been told they may sell. 'All the men are in the lodge,' we're told. They invite us in. After reading all the books about the Indians I'm surprised and honoured. Imagine a white woman invited into the men's council. I picture them sitting in a circle wrapped in blankets, with feathers and beads, passing around the peace pipe.

I have to laugh at myself when we enter to find the men sitting around watching a basketball game on the TV. They are very hospitable and we buy some beautiful jewellery which we carry away wrapped in a brown paper bag.

Saturday night in town and the Indians, who are not allowed by law to drink, are drunk. The sherrif's deputies drive down the main street with a flat-bed truck holding a cage into which they unceremoniously drop what is left of the great Indian nation.

Our trip to America ends at the edge of the sea on the magnificent California coastline at Big Sur and we return to London, where we live for several years.

'I'm not good enough for you,' he starts.

'Oh, Jamie.'

'No, really, I hate going out with you.'

'Why?'

'When we go into a restaurant, you're so beautiful everybody stares at you and then they look at me and say to themselves, "What's she doing with him?"'

Because Jamie loves very thin women, to please him, I practically live on coffee and cottage cheese, but I can never be thin enough for him. Sometimes I feel he would like me to be so thin I disappear completely.

We decide to get married so I go on ahead to my mother's in Palm Beach to plan the wedding. My mother and I have a wonderful time getting dolled up to go to lunch at the Colony and shop along Worth Avenue. Deciding what to wear for the wedding takes endless discussions, every detail must be perfect. We have fun spending a fortune on beautiful negligees and naughty underwear. I practise some new recipes, a carrot cake with cream cheese icing, which I know Jamie likes. I even take driving lessons and learn how to drive a car, sort of. 'Where'd ya get your licence, lady, in a Sears and Roebuck catalogue?' a truck driver shouts when I back into him.

My mother takes charge of the wedding. The reception is booked at the Poinciana Club, the room overlooking the water. A wedding cake covered with roses and lilies of the valley is ordered and Jean-Paul is coming for the wedding and a holiday with me beforehand.

As a wedding gift, mother buys me the most exquisite champagne-coloured lace suit. We take in the waist till I can hardly breathe. No matter, I want to look as beautiful as possible for Jamie. I'm so happy and excited, floating on a pink cloud.

As James is a Catholic, I decide to take instruction in Catholicism; maybe even get married in church. The local church refers me to a priest who is willing to instruct me; I make an appointment and go to the house where a group of priests are living together. They are sitting around drinking beer and watching TV. Somehow I had pictured them praying all day.

My teacher invites me to come into the office. 'Thank you, Father,' I say. He looks like he played football in college, maybe thirty-five years ago and hasn't exercised since, his breath reeks of whisky. As he talks, I realize he's a little drunk. 'Yes,' he confides in me. He has a drinking problem, has been sent to Florida to get help with it, so he has plenty of time to instruct me. I feel sorry for him. He's so empty, so basically lonely. But I don't feel like continuing.

Jamie arrives so late he almost misses his own wedding. The man I pick up at the airport is an entirely different person from the man I left in London a month and a half ago. Surly, uncommunicative, he hasn't even bothered to shave. He hardly speaks to me. Pre-wedding jitters, I think, and keep up a cheerful front, chatting away.

We are married by a judge in my mother's home. It takes me the whole morning to get dressed. When he sees me, Jean-Paul's eyes grow large, 'Oh, mommy, you look beautiful, like a fairy princess.' Jamie doesn't say anything, practically ignores me. Alone in the elevator, after the ceremony, he turns on me. 'This is the most unhappy day of my life,' he says bitterly.

After the reception, with everyone toasting our happiness, we go back to the hotel, where he lies down on the bed in his clothes and goes to sleep immediately. Quietly, so as not to disturb him, I sit down in a chair and wait. I wait all night in the beautiful lace suit, the roses wilting in my hair, trying to figure out what I've done wrong.

In the morning I ask him, 'Is it another woman?' 'No,' he swears it isn't. 'I love you,' he promises. 'Just give me some time.'

I'm sure things will be fine as soon as we get home – we've been so happy in Randolph Crescent. But they aren't. 'I'm not good enough for you. You should be with someone who's rich.' 'Oh, Jamie, I don't care about that. I want to be with you.' He tells me he wants me to give him more time, that he wants to live in his studio; when he is successful, he'll feel like a man and then he'll come back. There's no phone and he doesn't want me to visit him, but he comes to visit me every day and keeps telling me he loves me. So, I hang on hoping.

Then suddenly after six months he's back. We're happy for a few days, then one evening the phone rings. 'Is James there?' a woman asks.

'No, he isn't. Is there a message?' I ask.

'Yes, you can tell him I want my keys back.'

'Who may I say rang?'

'Annie.'

'Should I take your number?'

'He knows it,' she says sharply and hangs up.

It all falls into place and out. Jamie comes home in a good mood whistling. 'Hello, Kinkajoo. God, I'm starving; couldn't stop all day.' I watch him begin to make a sandwich the knife spreading the butter evenly. 'Any phone calls, little one?' he asks.

'Just one,' I say.

'Oh, who?'

'Annie! She wants her keys back.'

The knife stops mid-air. 'Oh, shit!!'

'Why don't you be honest, for once in your life!' I say.

'OK . . . but it meant nothing. I love you,' he answers.

'It meant nothing? That's even worse!'

The bell rings. It's her, demanding her keys, demanding James. My curiosity gets the better of me. I want to see her, size her up. I wonder, will she be very beautiful; very sexy I'm sure. She turns out to be very ordinary in looks and manner. My estimate of James goes way down. Only for one minute do my fingers itch to throttle her. 'Tea?' I ask politely. 'Thank you,' she says. We sit and talk about photography, ignoring James. I rather like her and I can't help noticing with delight that she has thick legs.

After she leaves I stand by the stove, shivering suddenly with cold. 'You see,' James says conspiratorially, 'No one can drive us apart.'

Something snaps in me. I pick up a plate and throw it at his head. It happens to have his dinner on it. It misses him, smashing against the wall. He jumps up. I throw myself at him screeching, scratching him, hitting at him. 'I hate you,' I scream.

Spent, I run into the bedroom and throw myself across the bed sobbing. He comes and takes me in his arms. 'Oh, Kinkajoo. Little Kinka. Don't you know I'm the only one who can hurt you, but I'm the only one who can comfort you, too.' 'Oh, Lion,' I say clinging to him, in tears, 'Goodbye, Lion.'

*   *   *   *

Alone again, I find myself with serious financial problems. First and foremost I have to find the funds to keep Jean-Paul in school. I consult Gabitas Thring and they suggest several alternatives. They put me in touch with a group of men who help extraordinary boys through school in the hope of them eventually entering the priesthood or making a spiritual contribution to the world.

I apply and a lovely man comes to visit. Of course, we aren't Catholics, or anything for that matter, but because Jean-Paul is attending a Catholic school – in fact he had gotten together a group of his friends and formed a religious study group – they took it for granted he was a good Catholic boy. Somehow he also got the idea I was a widow. Perhaps because when he asked about my husband, I turned my eyes skyward and said sadly, 'Gone'. Of course, I didn't say gone to Annie in Shepherd's Bush.

Proving Jean-Paul is special isn't difficult. He has already won two scholarships and by the time he is twelve is doing university-level music. I think he is the most wonderful person. He is always amazing me with his goodness, his character, his innate kindness. I tell the man a story of how Jean-Paul had tangled with the school bully. After beating up some of the smaller boys who couldn't defend themselves, the bully, a big fat boy, decided to pick on Jean-Paul. Jean-Paul told me, 'He hit me and I grabbed him and held him up against the wall. Really, Mom, I don't know where I got the strength. He's much bigger than me, but I held him there and I told him, "I won't hurt you, but someone else will if you don't stop".' The boy had stopped and become Jean-Paul's devoted follower.

He thought Jean-Paul was just the sort of boy they would like to sponsor; all he had to do was meet him for final approval.

I tell Jeany all about the meeting and about their hopes that he might become a priest. He looks at me and then with a little twinkle in his eye asks, 'You didn't sign me up for anything, did you, Mom?'

CHAPTER 6

There's no money, but there is a camera. Necessity breeds opportunity and in two minutes flat I become a photographer. I call Askews and Valerie sends over two models to be photographed.

She has a classic, haughty look. He's gorgeous, half-Jamaican, half-Scots. I drape her in yards of gold lamé and a king's ransom of jewellery Bee lends me. I undress him. 'Clothes are so dating,' I joke. We create a little scene together. 'Yes, bite her shoulder. Why not? Yes, look at me. Beautiful, beautiful. Move your head just a fraction to the right. Oh, my God, that's it. Don't move. If you could see how amazing you look.'

The finnicky English sun, as if on cue, casts a shaft of light into the studio. 'Quick,' I say, 'lie down on the floor.' 'What?' 'On the floor, on the floor. In that patch of sunlight. Please sun,' I pray, 'don't go away. Lean in to it more, more.' The gold lamé catches the light and shimmers up into her face. The jewels catch fire. He prowls in her shadow looking magnificent. It works. 'Yes! Yes! It's gorgeous. You're gorgeous!' My heart is pounding. Keep your hand steady, I remind myself. Hold it, hold it. Perfect.

I can't get the film up to Leith's to be processed fast enough. I run along the canal and arrive out of breath just before closing. When I explain what I want done with the prints he laughs at me. Amateur, he teases. 'You can't do that, lass.'

'You mean technically?'

'No, it can be done, but it's not good photography.'

'Yes, well do it anyway!' I say.

'Is that me?' gasps Heidi when I show her her pictures. She had come in depressed, with husband trouble, over-permed hair and a tight mouth from having to keep it shut. We scrape back her hair and throw a sequined veil over it, play with make-up and talk till she relaxes.

'You've made me beautiful.'

'No, I just recorded it. I don't retouch. That's how you can look.' A month later I meet her on the street looking like her photograph.

Because I've been on the other side of the camera I can understand the problems and insecurities. A beautiful girl wails, 'I hate my nose.' 'Not my left profile,' another says. They know I'm on their side.

I have so many pictures in my head, they are flowing out of my eyes. I do portraits of the talented, the beautiful and the famous. Working with Carolyn Cowan, an artist whose canvas is the human face I combine fantasy with reality to achieve super reality.

I take so long draping Zandra Rhodes in her fabrics

she falls asleep and I photograph her that way. 'Don't worry I fall asleep everywhere, fell asleep at a dinner party the other night,' she says.

The opera conductor, Patrick Libby. 'I can only give you half an hour,' he announces. 'You'll have to be quick about it.' Rushing, I jam the camera in the middle of the shoot. I press the wrong button in my distress and the back of the camera flies open, clouding the film and ruining the pictures. I print them anyway. 'I love it,' he says. 'How did you get that romantic effect? It looks like I'm walking through a fog.' 'Oh, much too technical to go into,' I reply straight-faced.

For a portrait of David Bell, who has the face of an angel, I decide to portray him as such. I find the most beautiful pair of large feathered wings at a theatrical costumier and bring them home to try on myself. They are ingenious. The straps that attach them to your body are invisible. The effect phenomenal. I'm admiring myself in the mirror when the doorbell rings. I'm surprised to see the gas man at the door; he looks surprised also. 'Here to read the meter, ma'am,' he says.

'Follow me,' I say as I walk down the hall, my wings bobbing gently behind me.

The Chenil Art Gallery is interested in giving me a show. The director comes to tea to look at my work. 'Yes,' he muses, 'I think I would like to show you.'

When he leaves I walk around the flat smiling, the smile enlarges, splits into a grin and bursts out laughing. Imagine me, the one who was only good for making tea or making love, having a show.

On 15 December 1981, my show 'Modern Icons' opens at the Chenil Gallery. There is an opening night party and all my friends come and celebrate. I look at the exhibition and see with satisfaction the large black and white prints graphically clean and knowing, lush colour portraits, repainted, gilded and jewelled into modern icons.

*   *   *   *

Though I love my work it's impossible for me to live without a man for long. The next disaster is the musician Hans Zimmer whose hit, 'Einstein-a-go-go' is in the charts and will be nominated for an Oscar for the score from *Driving Miss Daisy*, another tortured German, master of angst. He lives surrounded by synthesizers with his dog Woofer. 'Get me something to eat,' he calls after me, 'Something unhealthy.' I stop by his place after a party wearing black satin and lace. 'You should be punished for looking like that,' he says and he does.

I'm beginning to hate the words, 'I love you'. Words, only words. So many kinds of words, some flattering, like a fat *marron glacé*, pop quickly from the mouth in a burst of sugar sweetness. The silly words, like spaghetti, giggly with sauce. So many luscious words to feast on but there are also the words I can't bear, knife words, the murderous meat red words that say no . . . go!

How many times will I make my bed? And how many times lie in it and call it love. In the world's eyes I am privileged, but fate and time will peel good fortune from my frame, will pluck the wild fruit. Soon who will want me? Women are such perishable goods.

I've pushed at all the doors, rattled the handles and called out. Labouring so long to be born.

*   *   *   *

'Mom, I'm home,' Jean-Paul calls out. Back from visiting his father in Amsterdam, he's bursting with news. 'When I was sitting my final exams I prayed to God and said I would give my life to Him. Then, when I was visiting my father, I met that English devotee, you know him, on the street and he took me to the temple and preached to me, so I've decided not to go to university and become a doctor. I'm going to join ISKCON and become a devotee. Why should I spend my life treating the body, which is temporary, when I can treat the soul which is eternal?'

The idea doesn't thrill me. 'Couldn't you go to school and still be a devotee?' I ask, 'or finish school and then become a devotee.' No, he's made up his mind. He's like a rock. I can see there's no point in forcing him and anyway I doubt that I could; besides I'm not so sure he's wrong. He has the courage of his convictions, the purity of intention. 'Put not your trust in things which moth and rust doth corrupt. Besides,' he adds, 'with you for a mother, what else could I be?'

CHAPTER 7

A young monk stands before me, in saffron robes, his head shaved as a sign of renunciation, except for a small tail at the back called a *sikha*, his body marked with *tilak*, clay from the sacred river Ganges in twelve places for different names of God. My son's face is shining with love and his love is pulling at my resistance. 'Come to the temple,' Animisha is saying. I don't really want to. It's different now.

Since Srila Prabhupada's death in 1975, ISKCON, the International Society for Krishna Consciousness, which he had founded, has been managed by a governing body consisting of twelve gurus, each with authority over a different zone.

The guru for England is an American called Jayatirtha. His soft eyes peer gently from behind his glasses at me. 'I hear you are interested in Krishna consciousness,' he says. 'Yes, I am,' I answer. He looks like he's thinking about how humble he is. Scepticism rises like nausea in my throat. I miss Prabhupada.

In the twelve short years of his preaching mission Srila Prabhupada had travelled fourteen times around the world to open over a hundred centres and to initiate 6,000 disciples. The 'Hare Krishna' mantra had been a hit record, the devotees appearing on *Top of the Pops* and George Harrison singing it at an aid concert for Bangladesh.

From the very beginning it had been a risk. His body had been sick, an old man's body. Going to America, on the Jaladhuta he had suffered two heart attacks, but the spirit and the will were healthy. He was Krishna's and it shone out of eyes that had thousands of expressions, that looked into you and saw you through all the nonsense coverings; master of every mood, yet so humble you wanted to protect him.

He received the gifts of his followers graciously, looking at the love of the giver not the worth of the gift. He valued a paper garland made by one of the children of his disciples as highly as an expensive pearl ring. He wore the gifts for a while and then gave them away. He was not attached or even attracted to the world. 'This world is no place for a gentleman,' he told us.

He was patient with us, understanding how little we knew. Mukunda tells me a story about driving with Srila Prabhupada in the car, and Srila Prabhupada has an apple which he takes a bite out of. It's the Vedic custom that when the spiritual master gives the disciple the remnants of his food, it is considered purifying and helps you advance in spiritual life. It is a great honour to be given such a remnant. So Srila Prabhupada took a bite out of the apple and gave it to Mukunda. Innocently

Mukunda took a bite and passed it back.

When Srila Prabhupada founded ISKCON there was nothing, but very quickly riches came. Prabhupada taught that money in itself was not evil as long as it is used in the service of God. His Bhaktivedanta Book Trust became the largest publisher of spiritual books in the world. He built many beautiful temples, but, perhaps foreseeing the future, he told of how his spiritual master had told him at the end of his life after building sixty-four *maths* or temples in India, to see his disciples fighting over the properties. 'I should have taken the marble off the walls and put it into books.' And it's the books which last, the ancient scriptures translated into all languages carrying the message of God forward past all the frailties of man.

At the end Prabhupada wanted to be in Vrndavana, the village in India of Krishna's appearance, for his death. He struggled with his body to the very last, giving everything. The doctors couldn't understand how he was still alive, much less working so hard.

His leaving was unbearable. His senior devotees came to his bedside in tears. 'Srila Prabhupada, you can't leave us now. We aren't ready.' They had given deep thought to their request. The eyes fluttered open. 'The voice is weak, but if you need me to stay, I will.'

'Please stay,' they beg.

'Bring me some *prasadam* then.' By the afternoon he was sitting up and shouting orders. The devotees were reprieved, but even for him the time came when he had to leave us. He was so thin, his eyes oceanic, as the devotees carried him down to the temple to see the deities, though he was too weak to give class.

The devotees gathered around his bed chanting and praying as they were doing in temples all around the world. Now Srila Prabhupada who had taught so much, had to teach the devotees how to die. He had given them the knowledge of eternal life and now he showed them how to meet the death of the body. *'Engage your mind always in thinking of Me, become my devotee, engage your body in My service and surrender unto Me. Completely absorbed in Me, surely you will come to Me.'* On the out breath of the holy name, his soul flew home to be again with his beloved Lord.

Usually in Hindu India, people are cremated, but the body of a spiritual master is buried, the place marked as a *samadhi*. The body is prepared and lowered into the earth. One of the younger disciples held the small feet. He cried and cried. Somehow he couldn't let go, as if by holding them he were still connected to his spiritual master. Now that he was gone, all the devotees must somehow hold on to him. It is written that after the death of the spiritual master, chaos will reign.

Six years after Srila Prabhupada's death, I am praying in the Temple. Fine-boned as a medieval miniature etched in ivory, double-columned and with cut-out and curli-cued mock Eastern windows, it hangs above a sleeping London. Outside, the grey Soho streets are littered with McDonald's wrappers, bits of broken glass, specks of vomit and a clamped car.

In an upper room, young monks with *chadars*[*] wrapped around them against the morning cold sit

* A blanket or cloth meant to cover the upper part of the body.

before the gorgeous Rhadha Krishna deities who have been dressed in sumptuous clothes, in silk and gold brocades and ornate jewellery, garlanded with fresh flowers which mix the aroma of gardenias and eucalyptus oil.

They have been warned. 'If you want many beautiful women, great riches . . . do not look at that beautiful boy Krishna who is playing his flute on the bank of the river Jamuna.'

But it is too late. The chink of the Kartals pierces the air, cleaning it, and the drone of the harmonium swims into the song. They sing about the pain of separation from their Lord, while the *mridangas** hold down the beat.

They've been up since four for *Mangal Artik*,† to chant their rounds, hands in beadbags, pulling 108 wooden beads through their fingers, concentrating on the sound vibration, 'and the word was with God, and the word was God. Dear Lord,' they pray. 'Let me serve you.'

Class begins with a reading of the Sanskrit text, followed by the English translation, then Srila Prabhupada's purport, which is followed by the speaker's own analysis of the *sloka*'‡ and then questions or comments by the devotees. In Bhakti Yoga, there is no mental speculation. The final authority is always Krishna. Real religion, Srila Prabhupada taught, is not man-made, but comes from God alone and man must try to understand

---

* Elongated, two-headed sacred drum used in kirtan and bhajan (devotional or religious music).
† First worship ceremony of the day, observed before sunrise and considered specially auspicious.
‡ Verse.

and follow the word of God, 'Not my will, but Thy will, Lord.'

Is it possible that I've heard these words before in different bodies at different times, looking through different coloured eyes; blue, green, brown and blind eyes. Weighed down by ideas and histories that have clung to the soul from the beginning of time, material debris that stuck to it obscuring this voice, till it was muffled by a thousand painful distractions, lost in the strident screeching of the world and its needs that were never really needed.

'Let he who has ears hear,' and Krishna says in Bhagavad Gita*. *'For the soul there is neither birth nor death. Nor, having once been, does he ever cease to be. He is unborn, eternal, ever-existing, undying and primeval. He is not slain when the body is slain,'* and hearing, my heart bursts inside my chest and joy fills me. At last the dragon of death is slain, the scales of illusion fall from its ugly body and it is powerless to stop me as I pass out of the desert of death and start my journey home.

My heart may be filled with joy, but my body and emotions are in turmoil. I need to train my body to sit still and cross-legged yogi fashion on the floor for the entire class, but at first I can only sit this way for a few minutes before my knee joints pull apart. Yet every day I force myself till by the end of the month, I'm able to concentrate fully on the class instead of on my complaining body.

Staying awake is even more difficult. I'm not used to

* The discourse between the Supreme Lord Krishna and his devotee Arjuna, expounding devotional service as both the principal means and the ultimate end of spiritual perfection.

rising at 3 am and I find I must walk up and down to chant my rounds or I fall asleep. Class becomes an agonizing fight between my painful body and the need to sleep. I'm not alone in this. All over the temple room you can see exhausted young devotees nodding off during class.

One day a guest comes to visit the temple and hear class. After class he is filled with excitement. 'I want to join right away,' he says. He tells his friend, 'I've never seen anything like it. They open a big book and begin to read and I actually saw some of them go into a mystic trance right there and then!'

Even though I've seen that material life has a low profit margin, I'm afraid to take the plunge to commit myself to becoming a devotee. If I venture out into this ocean, will I fall off the edge of the world? I'm burning but I can't let go. So I lie on my bed feeling myself pulled in opposite directions, feeling my insides rip and membrane stretch till it will tear, knowing if I can't let go I'll damage myself, but I can only lie here hugging a pillow to my body waiting for the pain to pass, wait it out, wanting both. The world and God.

What I fear most is the vow of celibacy. Sex is allowed only in marriage and then only once a month for the propagation of children. Having three lovers and a husband at present, I have long discussions with the devotees about it. I feel passions are somehow holy, but the teaching says it is lust and the only pure love is love of God. They've obviously never been in love, I think. So we argue back and forth.

'Why three lovers?' Mondokini's husband asks me. 'I want to love purely and with only one I become too attached, too insecure.' 'Why not seven then?' he laughs, 'one for every day of the week.' 'I'm working my way up to it,' I laugh back. But in my heart I know they are right, that what I am looking for, have always been looking for, is God.

'You remind me of St Augustine,' says Hamsadhutta. 'Oh?' I say, flattered by the comparison. 'Yes,' he says. 'St Augustine used to pray, "Oh, Lord, save me, but not today. Let me sin a little longer".'

Soon I'm working down in the kitchen of their vegetarian restaurant called Healthy, Wealthy and Wise. All day long I wash up for the cooks, my hands in warm soapy water, getting all the black marks off the big pots, scrubbing away till they gleam, singing for myself mantras and spiritual songs I've learned from the devotees, washing and cleaning till I feel clean and fresh and good-humoured myself.

News of my mother's arrival in London is met with mixed emotions by Animisha and myself. She doesn't know we've become devotees and we don't think she'll be overjoyed at the idea. She arrives looking as glamorous as ever and arranges to take us to lunch at a fashionable restaurant at the Inn on the Park. Animisha, I mean Jean-Paul, arrives and I go to open the door for him to find he's hidden his shaved head with a blond bubble wig. 'For God's sake, Anni, that's a girl's wig,' I hiss, before breaking into hysterical laughter.

'I know,' he whispers back, 'but it's all I could afford. The men's wigs cost a fortune.'

I try to press it down but the acrylic curls keep springing back up.

'Hey, you two,' my mother calls, 'what's all the

whispering out there?'

'Oh, nothing,' we say in unison.

She gives her grandson a hug seeming not to notice that his hitherto straight brown hair has become a mass of blond curls.

'I'm starved,' she says. 'Let's go to lunch.'

At lunch we order vegetarian food and Animisha says the prayers under his breath. 'Is that all you're going to eat?' she sighs. Anni gives a violent sneeze and his wig slips back a few inches on his forehead and puffs out at the base of his neck. It now looks like he's wearing a rather strange hat. I don't dare to look at him any more. 'You're catching cold,' my mother says. 'And no wonder, the way you eat!'

We want to introduce her to our spiritual ideas gradually, so we decide that we will play the 'Hare Krishna' mantra quietly in the background as just by hearing it she will become purified. Everything is going nicely till she leans over and snaps off the tape machine. 'That rock and roll,' she says, 'it's so repetitive!'

*　*　*　*

Sunday, and I haven't gone to the morning programme at the temple. Sleep and a strange reluctance have kept me at home. In the studio shafts of sunlight breathe lacy patterns on the walls and the quiet is pricked by children's laughter from the garden below. I'm enjoying the pleasure of paint, working on the photographic illustrations for a planned book of poetry by a young devotee named Padmapani.

Photographic colours are never intense enough for me, so I'm painting in a sky, violet-tinged and so thickly blue that the eye is soothed in its milky depths. Then the phone rings. It seems that the guru for England, Jayatirtha, has left ISKCON and formed a breakaway group. He's gone completely off the deep end, even advocating the use of LSD. He calls it the sacrament, to devotees who have taken a vow of no intoxication, no liquor, drugs, cigarettes or even tea or coffee. His followers love him and sentimentally follow him, foolishly not hearing the Vedic injunction that when a guru no longer acts as a guru should, he must not be followed. In the grip of hysteria they barricade themselves in a house and refuse to listen to reason. Animisha is with them.

I go out to the house but they aren't letting anyone in. I shout and shout. I'll shout down the walls if I have to, determined to speak to him. Finally, they send him out. 'Please don't go with them,' I plead. I'm sure they are going to join Jayatirtha who is in Navadwip, India.

'He's into drugs,' I say.

'That's blasphemy.' Animisha answers furiously.

'The truth is never blasphemy,' I argue back.

'It isn't the truth; the other gurus are jealous of him.'

It's the first time we've ever really fought. In desperation I get down on my knees in the mud. 'I beg you, Animisha, don't go with them. You'll ruin your spiritual life.'

'All right, I won't,' he promises, but two days later, the house is deserted and they are all in India.

To commit murder is a heinous crime. To kill the spirit is worse. When a so-called guru breaks his own vows, it is one thing, but when he takes his followers to hell with him it is considered the most awful crime imaginable, bringing with it dire consequences.

A little over five years later, Jayatirtha's body is found by police in a London store front, hacked to pieces by one of his disillusioned followers. The boy is also found sitting beside what is left of his spiritual master, covered in blood, hopelessly insane.

Now I can only think about Animisha. I have faith in his common sense and his sincerity, and I'm proved right. As soon as he arrives in Navadwip he sees it for what it is. The whole thing becomes an adventure. He decides that since he has the good fortune to be in India, he will make a pilgrimage to Vrndavana.

Without money to cross the continent he is forced to sell off his possessions, one by one. His wristwatch, his walkman, his *chadar* all gone when he is stricken with amoebic dysentery. Alone, in the middle of India in a sweltering room, he lies on the floor in his own vomit and excrement too sick to get up, even to go to the bathroom. Already thin, he looks like a skeleton when he finally reaches Vrndavana. He has lost so much weight and so much pride. He will come back better, humbled and greatly advanced. In spite of everything India has been good to him.

While Animisha is still in India, the most powerful guru in ISKCON arrives. He acts more like an emperor than a holy man, but his charisma is undeniable. I secretly spy on him conferring with his men, through a window at the top of a door sitting on the stairs, hidden from view, or so I think – until he sends the temple president, Rohini, to get me. 'Srila Gurudeva wants to meet you.'

'Well, I don't want to meet him. I've had enough of these gurus,' I say exasperating him.

'Please . . .'

'Oh, all right,' I agree.

Meeting Srila Gurudeva I discover a very charming man with a sense of humour which makes me laugh. Suddenly intense he asks, 'Are you really serious about spiritual life?' His blue eyes bore into mine.

'Yes, I am,' I say.

'Come with me, then, and I'll teach you myself.'

'When?'

'Now!'

I'm dumbfounded as is everyone else in the room.

'Get your things together,' he says, giving me his garland.

And it is with him that I am finally able to surrender, to say yes to God.

I take formal initiation; vowing to chant, to study scripture, to be vegetarian, to give up intoxication, illicit sex, gambling and mental speculation.

For Vyasa Puja, the birthday celebration of the spiritual master I write.

In the cool violet dawn of the Brahma Muhurta* you appear on the field of battle surrounded by your generals like the sun risen in a night of stars.

In the iron times of Kali's Yuga† , in need of heroes, a time when destiny meets illusion and mirage is the miracle of the moment, where happiness and distress is all distress. You train your soldiers to give up false ego's

---

* One and a half hours before sunrise considered particularly auspicious for meditation and self-realization.

† Present age, which began 5,000 years ago and lasts in total 432,000 years. Fourth, and last in a repeating cycle is the Iron Age – an age of quarrel and hypocrisy.

eccentricities, the defence of fear, the water weapons of tears, the anger of power. All things material being im- material to the coming battle. What alchemists art for changing base metal into gold.

He teaches me everything from the basics of wearing a sari ('Do I have to?') and tying my hair back, to Vedic philosophy in its purest and most sublime form.

Most of the time he is patient, elucidating spiritual knowledge, unfolding mysteries, straightening out what I have made complicated. I begin to realize that spiritual life is simple, it is I that am complicated and complicating. He tries very patiently to straighten me, to simplify me, to overcome the conditioned resistance of a mind which is like a frightened bird tangled in a net of illusion. 'You're one of a kind,' he jokes over my inadequacies, 'but your heart's in the right place.' He calls me his daughter.

Very occasionally his anger flashes like lightning across my darkness, illuminating myself for me.

'I've been thinking about your service,' he says one day as we sit in his room at the manor. It's winter and he wraps himself in a *chadar* of the finest cashmere as he speaks.

'I like washing the pots. It's very peaceful and I'm working on a book of photos and poetry with Padma-pani.'

'Hm,' he looks at me thoughtfully. 'Why don't you give your camera away?' he suggests.

My heart stops beating, 'My camera?'

'Yes, I want you to do a different service,' he says, drawing out the suspense.

'What do you want?' I ask weakly.

'I want you to preach – for me and with me.'

'But Srila Gurudeva, I'm not qualified!'

'Then get qualified!' he answers firmly, finishing the conversation.

Devastated, I go into Srila Prabhupada's room. The room has been kept exactly as it was when he was alive. I sit down in front of his desk, where I sat when he encouraged me to try and keep trying. I can feel his presence encouraging me now. 'Oh, Srila Prabhupada,' I say tears coming to my eyes. I want to follow, but this is too difficult. I remember Gurudeva once saying, 'I will drag you back to God kicking and screaming all the way if necessary.'

Depressed, I go downstairs to take *prasadam* with the devotees. 'I wish I was beautiful,' says one of the girls at the table, 'then I could spend hours with the spiritual master, too.'

Any problems I have are put aside when Animisha arrives home safely from India. We hug and hug each other and sit up all night talking about India, his realizations, the politics of ISKCON. Of course, I tell him all about Gurudeva.

We take a solemn vow to always help each other to advance in spiritual life. We can see there will be many problems from ourselves and from others. Many people, even those closest to us may not understand and through ignorance be prejudiced.

We are still laughing about the doctor we had gone to see. When he saw Anni's robes and shaved head, he got an expression on his face as though he smelled something bad. He is so rude that when he turns his back we stare at each other in mock horror. 'You're too thin,' he snaps, 'must be that vegetarian nonsense. How tall are you?' he asks, 'Five feet eleven?'

'Well,' says Anni, 'I was six feet two when I came in.'

In spite of everything he's as zany as ever. 'You think you've got problems,' he jokes, 'I'm wearing a dress and my friends call me Anni.'

The worry about Gurudeva's order to preach is put to the back of my mind as I have to go to Palm Beach to visit my mother.

*   *   *   *

Palm Beach is another world, a small strip of land between the Atlantic Ocean and the Intracoastal Waterway choc-a-bloc with millionaires' mansions and vacation condos whose trees stand to attention in pots of shadow on baize lawns. In Café L'Europe, azaleas surround a mosaic of delicacies as ladies in designer dresses lunch on Perrier and nouvelle cuisine, their faces uptight with plastic surgery. On the newsstands at Publix, tabloid headlines scream, 'James Dean is alive' or 'Man grows breasts' to 'inquiring minds'.

'Say hello to the Marquesa,' my mother says handing me the phone. 'Hello, darling. How are y'all,' she drawls. The Marquesa comes from Texas. Before I can answer, she launches into a tirade about how spiritual she is, her medical problems, how nobody understands her. 'I'm just too sensitive for this world.' Without taking a breath she invites me to a get-together at her house of 'very high spiritual people'. We meditate together, send out love vibrations to the world. 'Are y'all still so gorgeous?'

'Well, I . . .'

'Are y'all still modelling?'

'No, I'm a Hare Krishna.'

'What? Not those people at the airport?' The pause is long enough and cold enough for ice to form on the telephone wires. 'Well, come anyway,' she says magnanimously.

I arrive to find the group sitting in a circle around a candle. 'Now all take hands,' the leader, a bearded man in a smock instructs, 'and send your love out to the world.' I'm terrified I'm going to giggle in embarrassment. After only three minutes, they begin talking. After all, how much love can the world take. They mix a bit of philosophy with a bit of religion, with a whole lot of California, picking and choosing whimsically with no basis in scripture, discipline or reality. They are the kind of people who always say, 'You're a Scorpio, right?' when you're a typical Virgo; who tell you they were Egyptian royalty in their last life, making you wonder why no common people like bakers, or street sweepers are ever reincarnated.

Sitting, silently listening, a part of me jumps up thinking devilishly how I could, with logical argument, wipe the floor with them. But another voice overrides it saying, 'Look behind the facade, look with your heart and see how they are suffering and searching. Look with compassion and by the way a little humility wouldn't hurt either.' I look and see. My heart does melt for them.

Only out of politeness does the Marquesa ask what I think. 'It's not what I think but this is what Vedic philosophy says.' Inspired I speak as I have never spoken before giving all credit to Srila Gurudeva. At the door the Marquesa grasps my hand, 'I need help,' she says pressing so hard her rings cut into my flesh. 'If I come to London, can I meet the spiritual master?' Delighted, I give her a hug, 'Yes, of course!' I say.

CHAPTER 8

'Whatever action a great man performs, common men follow. And whatever standards he sets by exemplary acts, all the world pursues.' If the powerful people, the wealthy, leaders in society like the Marquesa take an interest then surely others will be attracted.

I go back to England and Gurudeva bursting with the news, 'So you've begun to preach,' he says smiling at me.

'Only by your Grace, Srila Gurudeva. Without you I could do nothing.'

'Yes,' he agrees.

'The Marquesa is coming and would like to meet you.'

'Can you arrange a luncheon?' he asks.

'Oh, yes.'

'Good, Bhumi can cook.'

The luncheon is held in the beautiful dining room at

Aldenham. The devotees serve up thalis* full of delicious *prasadam*. Srila Gurudeva sits at the head of the
table surrounded by his men, stalwart devotees and
sanyasis in the renounced order of life. There has been a
kirtan and the children from the *Gurukula* performed.
Srila Prabhupada taught that the education of children
was of paramount importance and set up schools called
gurukulas for the children of his disciples.

'Aren't they jus' too darlin',' gushes the Marquesa.

They discuss vegetarianism and charity. 'Ah, give
away so much.' 'Ah've got the money, ya know,' she
winks, 'from ma first husband.' She's especially interested in celibacy. 'Now Gurudee,' she begins, mis-
pronouncing his name. 'Ah'm renounced, too, ya know.
Ten years ago I said to the Marquis, "Honey! We're
gonna get spiritual! So no mo' foolin' around." And ya
know what? He agreed, jus' like that!' she pauses
thoughtfully. 'Ya know that kinda worried me, his
agreeing so fast.'

As she rattles on I cringe at the end of the table. Srila
Gurudeva's eyes meet mine. He looks amused.

After she leaves Gurudeva calls me into his room.
'That was very nice. She's really a character. These
people are very spoiled and need a great deal of
patience, but they can be very helpful to us. You carry
on. Keep bringing them to me.'

I go out fishing, meeting as many people as possible,
speaking to them about Krishna consciousness and inviting them back to Randolph Crescent which has
become a preaching centre.

* Indian metal dinner plates.

Every day around noon people start arriving, sometimes just one person and sometimes a group. We listen to *kirtan* and then have Bhagavad Gita class before tucking into a simple vegetarian meal. Over lunch we discuss philosophy often with a visiting *sanyasi*.

Mukunda Maharaja, who has taken *sanyasa* and is now the head of ISKCON's public relations, brings people and takes me with him when he goes out preaching. I try to be very careful about etiquette, for it is a Vedic injunction that a *sanyasi* should never be alone with a woman, not even his sister or mother. For the higher ideal of preaching, however, we sometimes mix, but very carefully. So when he picks me up in the car, I ask him, 'Should I sit in the back seat, Maharaja?' 'What? You want to be chauffeur driven?' he asks.

I invite him to stop by on Saturday to see our cooking class. Nobody ever cooked like Bhumi. She's the Genghis Khan of cuisine. She assaults the kitchen throwing ingredients everywhere. Some even get into the pot. I tell her, 'After your class cleaning the kitchen isn't enough. I have to repaint.'

Unfortunately, Mukunda stops by on the Saturday when Bhumi has set the kitchen on fire. He peers into the smoky room, sees everyone laughing and coughing and Bhumi slapping at the stove with a wet towel. 'Uh, yes,' he says, 'very interesting classes you two are giving.'

* * * *

'Out of many thousands among men, one may endeavour for perfection and of those who have achieved perfection, hardly one knows Me in truth.'

I find this *sloka* from Bhagavad Gita hard. In my heart I believe everyone can come to God, must come.

Gurudeva tries to help me. 'Not everyone is ready to become a devotee, but if they help the devotees, they become purified. Srila Prabhupada said even by appreciating one can make advancement. 'Be patient, Rytasha,' he says. But I hate this suffering world, this ignorance; I think, if they're so thirsty, why don't they drink?

But I know why. The fault lies not in them, but in me. My personality is like a disease, infecting everything. If only I was pure . . . But I can bring them to one who is.

I arrange elaborate dinner parties, mixing the guests with devotees. A judge may sit next to Sarah Miles, a businessman beside Sir John Mills. We use the best crystal, with luxuriant flowers and wonderful *prasadam*. After dinner there is entertainment, a play telling a Krishna story, a rock opera of the Bhagavad Gita, a concert of Indian music. One night rock stars Poly Styrene and Hazel O'Connor perform. Hazel sings a song she has written and which she dedicates to Srila Gurudeva. I do everything to make Krishna consciousness attractive, to break down any prejudices so they can hear the philosophy clearly. The centrepiece of the evening is Srila Gurudeva. The guests have the privilege of meeting him and hearing him speak. He invites questions and will often take a personal interest in someone who wants to learn and instruct them privately.

When Bhumi marries Sanjaya we decide it is the perfect opportunity to invite guests to see a Vedic wedding, with its fire sacrifice and feasting and to understand love and marriage in a spiritual context.

On a beautiful day, over a hundred guests are treated to fruit cocktails and *prasadam* on the Manor lawn. Then they begin to assemble in the temple room. Srila Gurudeva makes his entrance, but because of a mix-up in the arrangements, he isn't greeted properly. He goes to his room in a raging temper, tearing off his garland and refuses to come down so the ceremony can begin. The devotees are having a *kirtan* and the guests are seated and waiting. 'Is that the spiritual master?' one guest asks another, pointing to a life-size statue of Srila Prabhupada seated on the *vyasasan*. 'I think so,' his friend answers. 'He hasn't moved a muscle since we came in,' he whispers. 'Oh yes, they're yogis. They can do that.'

Bhumi is looking wonderful in the traditional reddish sari. In the East they wear red for marriage. White is the colour of death, worn by widows and renunciates. As the time goes by Sanjaya begins to look worried. Seeing his expression a guest wonders if they are being forced to marry; arranged marriages and all that.

The pujari* has made a small fire in the centre of the room and is chanting the prayers. The guests are given grains to throw into the fire; and still Srila Gurudeva doesn't appear and the *kirtan* bangs on and on till Princess Elizabeth of Yugoslavia turns white with waiting. 'I've got to get out of here soon if nothing happens.' Eventually Srila Gurudeva comes down and reluctantly marries them. 'Did you notice the gold rolex he was wearing?' someone asks over the wedding feast that follows.

* Priest.

* * * *

Srila Gurudeva can't always be in England. He must travel to his other zones such as France, Italy, Spain and South Africa, so he leaves me in the care of his right-hand man. Maharaja is very dear to him and it's easy to see why. He preaches like an angel, albeit an American angel and when he sings and plays the *vina*,* it is like being in the presence of Narada Muni, the celestial singer. I am delighted to have him for my spiritual authority, to learn from him and to work with him. Because of Srila Gurudeva I feel happy and secure for the first time in my life.

We do many wonderful programmes together, some very serious and some very funny.

Once we are seated at the same table at a ball given by Lady Lothian. On his place card they have put 'Swami'.† 'And you must be Mrs Swami,' says the man on my left, not realizing that 'swami' means celibate among other things.

Another time we are at the film director Tony Palmer's house discussing a possible production of the epic *Mahabarata*‡ when he slips his feet out of his sandals. One of the women with us opens her eyes wide in astonishment. She can hardly wait to get me alone. 'My God, he really is a saint, walking on nails.' 'He may be a saint,' I laugh, 'but the nails are rubber, the sandals are Japanese massage sandals.'

He pushes and pulls me along, worries that I spend

---

* A stringed musical instrument.
† A person in the renounced order.
‡ The history of greater India compiled by Srila Vyasadeva.

too much time with non-devotees, or *karmis* as they are called. 'You can preach to them, but you can't be friends. You may give association, but you must not take it.' It seems one of the devotees had said, 'Rytasha can't tell a demon from a devotee.' 'They're not demons,' I snap back furiously.

Srila Gurudeva takes me travelling with him. I had better be austere travelling with *sanyasis*, I think, so I take only one small bag. When I meet them at the airport they are standing beside a mountain of luggage. 'Oh good,' says Maharaja when he sees I have no hand luggage and starts loading me down with their bags as if I was a donkey. 'Maharaja!' Gurudeva laughs, 'Stop that!'

We stop briefly in America where my mother gives several dinner parties to introduce Srila Gurudeva to her friends.

Influenced by the media sensationalism, their mood is sceptical. Most are more interested in the financial aspects of ISKCON, asking where the money comes from and where it goes, than in the spiritual, though some are genuinely interested and take home books and learn to chant.

Before he arrives, I brief my mother on the etiquette of greeting a spiritual master and a *sanyasi*. 'Now, Mom, don't try to shake his hand or touch him in any way. It isn't proper.' So you can imagine my surprise when, after the party, he goes to her and gives her a big hug, completely confounding me. He calls her *mataji*, a term of great respect. 'Did you hear, Mom?' I say later that evening, 'he called you *mataji*. That means mother.' 'Mother!' she says insulted. 'What's the matter? He thinks I've got no sex appeal?'

We go into Mexico where we stay in a beautiful villa in Acapulco as the guests of the actress Linda Christian. She arranges for Srila Gurudeva to speak on the most popular programme on Mexican TV, but at the last minute he decides to fly to California instead.

'You do it, Rytasha,' he says. 'What! me? Oh Srila Gurudeva!' 'You know the philosophy. You'll be fine,' encourages Maharaja. 'Pray to Krishna!'

On the morning of the interview I arrive at the television station to find that the devotees, not wanting to lose the opportunity for preaching, haven't told the host of the programme that Srila Gurudeva can't make it. 'Oh, it's OK,' they say. 'We told them you're Srila Gurudeva.' 'You what?'

In horror I hear them announce, 'and now the head of the Hare Krishna movement, her Divine Grace Srila Gurudeva.' 'Dasi' I say, servant of. 'Si,' he answers. 'I'm the servant of . . .' 'Si Srila Gurudeva.' He continues, in Spanish. Somehow we get through the interview. At the end of the interview he kisses my hand, '*Gracias*, your Divine Grace. Hare Krishna.'

When he hears the tape Gurudeva is pleased. 'You did very well,' he says and smiles at me. All my happiness, my life lies in that smile. It is said, 'if the spiritual master is pleased then Krishna is pleased.'

* * * *

Though a neophyte, I have the great honour of meeting Jamuna, of putting a face to the voice I had heard all those years ago in Paris with Wahundra, that voice of such purity and exalted spirit that my life had changed because of its call, never dreaming that we would one day become friends. Her wholesome face transparent with kindness, she invites me to lunch and to friendship. 'Wouldn't it be wonderful to work together,' she says.

Srila Prabhupada had wanted to put Jamuna on the governing board of ISKCON, but the men wouldn't have it. They didn't want a woman, refused a woman, forgetting that the first thing Srila Prabhupada had taught them was, 'We are not these bodies, but spirit soul, servants of God,' and that, 'we make our judgements based on qualifications, not on the bodily concepts of man, woman white, black, American Indian.'

Sitting snug, smug in their male hierarchies, they have grown deaf. Their kingdom is on earth, their rule is mundane, material, of the earth and like the earth, temporary. No woman ever will be pope or priest. Of course they can't stop women being saints, who fly high above the religious bureaucrats and bankers, the men who clothe their naked ambition in robes of renunciation . . . Women need protection, they say; keep quiet! says St Paul; in Purdah! say the Muslims; shave your head and sit in the balcony behind a wall! say the Jews; into the fire of your husband's death! say the Hindus; 'Never trust a woman or a politician,' says Chanyka Pandit.

'Women must be protected,' they say and the women ask, 'but who will protect me from my protectors?'

But Gurudeva is an exception, giving me protection and power at the same time. 'He gives her so much rope, sooner or later she will hang him,' someone prophesies.

*   *   *   *

Several nights a week I like to go down to the Embankment with some devotees and friends to distribute *prasadam* to the homeless who live on the streets.

From the back of a truck we serve out hot nutritious meals to about a hundred people a night, mostly alcoholics and drug addicts. Slightly crazy, filthy, lice-ridden and yet there is a sweetness in them, as if the world by stripping them of everything has left their hearts bare also.

A little Irishman, barely as tall as my shoulders, with a black eye and a cut lip grabs both my arms to steady himself. 'I'll protect you,' he slurs, 'if anyone gives you trouble, you just come to me!'

And it can be dangerous. In a little park where the meth drinkers congregate, we are warned one night not to go into the band pavilion where they sleep, as there has been a murder, 'stole his shoes, too' they complain, leaving the man's body; but where his head should be there is only a mashed pulp.

On the Embankment they sleep out in the street dormitory-style on cardboard boxes. God knows what they remember, of beds with clean sheets, of wives and sweethearts. It's strange to think of these men, sleeping in urine-stained trousers as once having been some mother's son, someone's darling baby boy.

And not all are here for lack of money. On one of the cardboard beds lies a woman in her fifties wearing a headscarf. It's unusual to see a woman here, so I heap a plate with rice and vegetables and a little salad and bring it over to her. 'Would you like some dinner?' I ask. 'Oh, thank you, my dear,' says a cultured voice, 'but I've already dined at my hotel.'

At Christmas, my boys, as I call them, surprise me

with a Christmas present. A fur coat; of course there is
very little fur left on the coat. 'We worried you might
catch cold,' they say.

* * * *

I appear on TV, on *Arena*, on German television, the
news, do an interview on the BBC. Newspaper articles
appear. 'I think it's amazing that Krishna should choose
you of all people to speak for him,' comments Maharaja.

I'm sitting with some guests in Srila Gurudeva's room,
when Anna Raphael walks purposefully into the room,
wearing forbidden shoes, followed by a camera crew
who proceed to set up and start shooting.

When I bump into her later in the week at the Soho
Street Temple, she tells me that when she looked at the
rushes of her film, she found the cameraman had concentrated on me instead of Srila Gurudeva. She found it
amusing to see this face constantly popping up on the
film. 'I think my cameraman fell in love with you,' she
laughs.

We click immediately and become firm friends. I love
her intellect, classically trained, and her irreverent
humour. We both enjoy the same wicked sense of fun.
Educated at Oxford with a doctorate from Yale, she had
been the only woman opera director in England. And
though she says she looks like Charles Laughton, she is
in fact lovely, with a wild mass of golden hair and an
Edwardian face. Ripe as fresh peaches with curiosity
and a passion for life which corresponds to mine.

She decides to make a film about me and the movement, which we jokingly call *Blazing Sandals*, but will
become *Persuaders* and earn us enmity and death

threats and her the 'Best Young Director' Award of 1986.

* * * *

The aftermath of one of our dinner parties finds Hazel O'Connor in tears. 'How could they do this? You promised,' she sobs. 'Hazel, what are you talking about?' I ask alarmed.

Animisha had met Hazel at Lady Lothian's Ball and, overcoming her dislike for devotees, with his charming persistence had introduced her to me and invited her to Randolph Crescent for lunch. Soon she was coming every day to study Bhagavad Gita.

Hazel had been a pop star in the seventies and then gone on to star in the film, *Breaking Glass*. She was trying for a comeback and working on a new album when we met. On the surface she was rough and tough, but inside terribly fragile. With Animisha and myself she finds warmth and friends who care for her well being. But it wasn't the same at the temple where she had problems with some of the female devotees, some jealousy. We discussed the problem of women and their relationship to each other. 'There are men, there are women and there are us,' she told me in conclusion.

'The press,' she rages, 'You promised, no press.'

'Yes, of course.'

'Well, Maharaja had a journalist there from the *News of the World*, the worst,' she chokes.

'Now calm down,' I say, 'I'm sure it will be all right; I'll call Maharaja and straighten it out.'

'Maharaja!' I start, 'What's going on? You promised no press for Hazel. Remember when we all had lunch

'Spiritual life is like water, it needs a vessel to carry it,
and that vessel is religion'.

His Divine Grace Srila Prabhupada with Jean-Paul age 7 – 'like the sun risen in a night of stars'.

Preaching on Mexican TV – 'I want you to preach for me and with me'.

'There is enough in the world for everyone's need, but not for everyone's greed'.

Above Boating in supplies during a flood in Bangladesh – 'our boat pulled on an undertow of despair'.

Below 25,000 fed in flood disaster in Bangladesh – 'and the food we give must be the mercy of God'.

Above Razzaque Khan – 'God has sent me to help you'.

Below Opening a school in Dhaka with (l. to r.) Ambassador Panni, Dr Miyan, Mr Islam – 'man's condition will never change until man is changed'.

The clinic – 'unless there is medicine, not only for the body, but for the spirit;
where is the care?'.

The leper colony – 'to be the humble servant of all God's servants'.

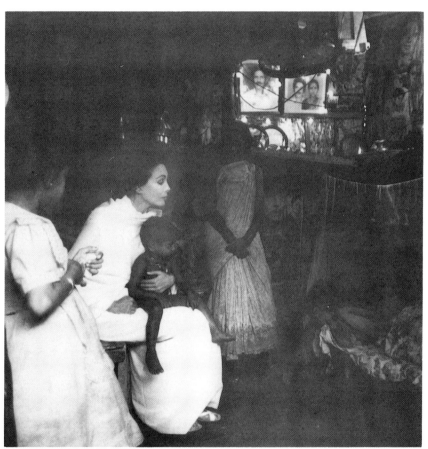

'40,000 children die of hunger, or hunger related diseases, every single day'.

'I will travel to a secret country to meet my Lord. There the fields are flat unto eternity and the sky is the colour of desire'.

together and Hazel said that she wanted to study and till she was certain she didn't want to go public and you promised to respect her privacy. This is all wrong, you can't just rip these people off.'

Maharaja is very abrupt. I've interrupted an important meeting with Srila Gurudeva and he doesn't like me telling him what he can and cannot do. 'Look, Rytasha, I'll handle things as I see fit,' he says and hangs up. This kind of thing happens too often . . .

The next thing I know Anna has decided to film the confrontation between Hazel, Maharaja and myself and has talked us all into it. How, I'll never know. I had started the film hoping it would be good PR for the movement but, as we filmed, things began coming apart at the seams and worst of all it was being recorded.

At the beginning I had said jokingly, 'Now Anna, I want you to portray me as very sweet and saintly,' and she answered, 'but, Rytasha, this film's supposed to be about you!' and we both had laughed. What makes Anna a brilliant filmmaker is that she looks for the truth of a situation and isn't afraid of it when she finds it. Now I am also being forced to look at the truth.

* * * *

God saw the suffering of the world and out of compassion said, 'I will give them religion'. And up popped the Devil saying, 'and I will organize it!' Purity is power and power attracts different kinds of people and different kinds of things in people.

Since Prabhupada's death the movement is increasingly taken over by administrators rather than saintly men. There is much jockeying for position and the perks that go with it. So-called renounced sanyasis sadhus demanding worship, glutting themselves on rich delicacies while the young pure-hearted *brahmacaris** worked their guts out on half-empty stomachs. There is much jet-setting accumulation of wealth, jewels and opulent living quarters. One guru caught having homosexual affairs is penalized by having his charge account at Bloomingdale's cut off. There are rumours of guns, drugs and child molestation.

But always there is the power of the teaching itself. God's perfection against man's fallibility. There are also the sincere devotees and they are in the majority, but it takes very little, and usually the little are very loud, to lose people's confidence. With only one match a great city may be destroyed.

'You're burning up, Rytasha,' Srila Gurudeva says. 'You should speak to me about it.'

But I can't. 'I promised myself I would only bring you sweet things, Srila Gurudeva.'

'Remember Rytasha, too many sweets make cavities.'

So I burn, smouldering with anger when the people I bring are spoken of in terms of what they can give instead of what we can give; when I see the young devotees collecting money all day, money that seems to disappear. They may call it *sankirtan*,† selling second-rate paintings, but to me, it's business and Srila

---

* A young celibate student aged 5 to 25, under the supervision of a spiritual master. This is the first of the four ashrams or spiritual orders of life.
† Congregational singing of the Holy Names of the Lord, but used in ISKCON for any activity furthering the movement.

Prubhupada didn't want us to be businessmen.

Even Animisha is getting frustrated. 'I'd like to sell books and preach,' he says, 'I'd like some independence in my service.' I'm angry when I see *sanyasis* who are supposed to have renounced the world, but have only moved up in the world and my anger must be apparent. With Maharaja it's carrot and stick. Sometimes he's kind, spending hours trying to help me, teach me, fine-tuning my service and sometimes it seems to me he's determined to break me, enlisting the devotees to help him do it.

He tells the temple president and his wife I want to take their position and where we had worked wonderfully together before, now a power pull is set in motion that involves the guests. Feeling threatened he becomes rude to me in front of my friends. He does childish things like changing the place cards around at the dinner table to assert his authority.

My phone is ringing. Look, my friends say, we respect your wishes for a spiritual life and we love to come to your house and have discussions, but we're worried about your being involved with these people. You'll get hurt, they warn. I find myself trying to explain the devotees to them, unsuccessfully.

Srila Gurudeva calls me into his room in a fury. 'You're fishing for big fish, Rytasha. Don't get pulled into the ocean. Bigger devotees than you are drowning in that ocean today,' he warns.

I try to explain that the devotees aren't acting like devotees, are actually hindering people in their spiritual life. 'I find that unbearable, Srila Gurudeva.'

'What's unbearable is your lack of humility.'

'Your duty is to please me and the devotees.'

'I want to do that,' I say. Tearfully I promise to try harder.

But I don't know how to straighten things out. Every move I make seems to make things worse. My programmes are cancelled or changed at the last moment and sometimes I'm even excluded from them entirely.

When my guests go in to have lunch with Srila Gurudeva, I'm stopped at the door. 'Oh sorry, I'm told there aren't enough chairs. You'll have to wait outside.' I'm put in charge of the parents programme and then Maharaja puts someone else in charge, not bothering to tell me. Going to the Embankment, I can no longer get a ride in the truck, after all they are all men; finally they stop the programme altogether.

I'm completely confused and frustrated, and break down in tears in front of Maharaja who sings to me, 'You look just like a woman, you make love just like a woman, but you break just like a little girl.' I'm furious with myself, because Gurudeva hates tears. 'Rytasha,' he says, don't act like a woman.' Anna says, 'They're afraid you're getting too powerful.'

In sleep I dream of Gurudeva. He is sitting in splendour high on a throne, but when I get closer I see he is playing jacks. Two high priests lead me up the stone steps where I kneel before him. They push my head down roughly on the stone three times, bruising my skin, forcing me against my will to pay my obeisances.

In dreams, on the rivers of the moon, the night currents are treacherous. High above the city of my mind, whose cinemas constantly show edited reruns of myself, high on the parapets of the fortress of me sit hideous gargoyles. They wear my face. They own my voice. 'You,' they shriek and their gnarled fingers point and prod. 'You sit at the table and eat, yet you condemn those you sit with. See how you twist and turn yourself to unnatural positions to suck illicit pleasures that serve not God.' Renunciation howls out of their mouths, their breath hot as fire. I squirm every which way on this spit of truth. My body sweats tears of anguish.

I get up from my bed, to look for the dawn. I know the night is blind. Soon the sun will rise and I will see. I will act and I will forget.

* * * *

Maharaja wants me on the street. 'She should collect, like any other devotee,' and Gurudeva agrees. 'It will help her to learn humility.'

Unwillingly, but because it is the order of the authorities I go out on to the streets to beg. I must find the courage to stop strangers, to ask them to give me something for the programme on the Embankment. I invite them to come down and help serve.

It's winter and the streets of London are freezing. No matter how warmly I dress, after a few hours the cold comes up through the pavement, chilling my feet and legs and up till it rests damply in my chest. Never physically strong, I am often sick, but I'm determined. Occasionally, reluctantly, I go into a café and drink some hot milk, cupping the glass in both hands to thaw out my frozen fingers.

My ego is in shreds. I feel ashamed to beg on the street, to be brushed aside, to have people avoid me, ignore me, look down on me. I'm afraid I'll meet someone who knew me from the old days, when I was a model. 'You'll never guess who I met today,' they will say to mutual friends, 'and you'll never believe what she was doing. She was begging on Oxford Street!' A young punk comes up to me and spits in my face. 'Go to hell!' he shouts.

I learn to overcome my fears by learning to forget myself, by remembering the poor people of the Embankment. I learn to think only of serving God, and I learn how truly kind and giving people really are. Most people, if they stop, will listen and give something. On Bond Street a well-dressed man stops and gives me £10. I'm amazed as people usually give change. 'A few years ago,' he tells me, 'I was on the Embankment myself.'

At the Reading Festival I sell books, mainly Bhagavad Gitas. I engage one young man in conversation and though he is stoned out of his mind he listens intently as I explain the message of the Gita.

Suddenly he looks at me as if he's been struck by lightning and throws himself to the ground in front of me, clutching my ankles and sobbing and screaming incoherently. 'Please, sir,' I say, stepping back trying to disengage myself, embarrassed as people turn to stare. 'Here, sir. Please, sir. Here have the book. It's a gift.' Still he continues to wail till his friends drag him away, clutching the book.

I'm not so lucky with the Hell's Angels, either, who when I approach them, throw me to the ground threatening and mocking me. When I see the books all over the ground, fear is replaced with anger. 'How can you act like this?' I say, red-faced with fury. 'You should all pay double for these books.' Incredibly, meek as lambs, they buy a book and give a nice donation.

Begging on Oxford Street there is a persistent tapping on my shoulder. 'One minute,' I say. 'I'm just speaking to this gentleman.'

'Now!' says a hard voice.

I turn to find a policeman.

'You're under arrest,' he says. 'Come with me,' he orders holding my arm tightly, so I can't run away.

'Oh, Krishna,' I whisper under my breath.

'Shut up,' he says.

When we get to the police station I'm booked and taken into a room by two large policewomen. 'Undress!' they order.

'What?!'

'Take off your clothes. Hurry up!'

Slowly I take off my coat and sweater.

'C'mon, c'mon!'

I get down to my underwear.

'All of it!'

I stand in front of them naked.

'Now turn around. Keep turning. Slowly,' they say, enjoying themselves. 'OK, that's enough. Get dressed and sit over there.'

I wait, feeling exhausted, when an officer comes in. 'Hello,' he says to me.

'You know her?' he's asked.

'Sure, she feeds the people down on the Embankment.' Turning to me, he says, 'That's a really nice thing you're doing.'

They let me go then, but I'm charged with obstruction, blocking the street, and must appear in court to pay a fine. In the hallway outside the courtroom, I meet the policeman who arrested me. He comes over. He seems embarrassed, worried. 'You know, it's within our rights to take away your clothes. We have to make sure you can't commit suicide.' I look at him, in amazed disbelief, hoping he hears himself sound so foolish.

* * * *

On a trip to Italy I approach Srila Gurudeva with an idea. I want to set up a programme to distribute *prasadam* in disasters. I want to go to the poorest countries, Africa, Ethiopia, the Sudan, Bangladesh, wherever the need is the greatest.

'You, Rytasha?' he laughs, 'dressed like that, with those ear-rings?' We are doing a dinner and I'm wearing a chiffon sari trimmed in gold and rhinestone ear-rings almost to my shoulders. 'Of course not!' I say. 'Rytasha, you can barely cook for two and now you want to cook for two thousand?' The men in the room join in his laughter. You may laugh, I think, but I'm going to do it. 'I'll organize it,' I say, 'but you will be the head of it, then when you preach people will respect you.' 'Well, it might be good, but it will be hard work. You'll have to go from one disaster to another.' 'No problem, Srila Gurudeva,' I say, 'I've been doing that all my life!'

CHAPTER 9

Not knowing I've left, I leave, journeying to the mystic East, where time contains the eternal pastimes. Here Lord Krishna still sings to Arjuna at Kuruksetra,* in the valley of Ajalon Joshua commands the moon to stand still, Jesus at the pool of Siloah cures a man born blind, and while the prophet Mohammed travels to the seventh heaven, the Buddha sits under a bo tree already there.

'Go to Bangladesh,' says Abhirama, a devotee friend from Key West. 'I have a friend Vyasiki who will help you.' Animisha, who knows India, warns me. 'Don't drink the water. Don't eat anything on the street. Don't forget to get your shots and take your malaria pills.'

I expect it will be difficult. I'm prepared for the harsh realities of going to one of the poorest countries in the world. I'm not prepared to fall in love with it.

---

* The battlefield on which Krishna taught Arjuna the Bhagavad Gita.

Arriving in Bangladesh, I'm hit by a wall of heat and streets teeming with life. Driving through Dhaka in a bright blue rickshaw, decorated with gooey-eyed movie stars, with mythical birds and Christmas trim, the rickshaw wallah keeps turning to look at me. I look back smiling, studying his open face, the skin drawn tight across his cheek bones, a brightly coloured cloth wrapped around his black hair glossy with mustard oil, his fingernails lacquered a bright red. He pedals barefoot past soldiers stationed every few feet around the city enforcing Martial Law, just declared, pedals quickly through narrow alleys smelling of incense and urine, past markets with pyramids of oranges, horny-skinned jackfruit and apples from India, where a man sits fanning a mound of dates, scattering a black cloud of flies.

Because he keeps turning to look at me, we nearly hit another rickshaw carrying two Hindu women in gossamer saris. We bump over railway tracks, along whose rails run the *bustees*, camps of slums, a scab of makeshift houses of rag and stick. A Muslim woman in a black *burkha** lifts her veil to peek at us. As we wait at a traffic light a herd of goats is driven through the streets, clipping away through their last day on earth. On the pavement a man stands next to a bathroom scale weighing people for a few *poisha*† and next to him an astrologer with long hair claims to know your future.

Life is lived in the open, on the street. Men sit in shops piled high with saris. Fixed price, they lie – eventually everything is negotiable. People bathe in the street, fully dressed, dumping buckets of water over

* The all-covering gown worn by some Moslem women.
† Small change in Bangladesh.

themselves. Barbers shave and cut on the street under a yellowing picture of Lord Siva[*], the moon in his hair, a snake around his neck. They even pray in the street, on prayer mats, five times daily.

On Tejukuni Para three beggars are walking in a row, holding hands. Two are blind led by a third, a cripple, who limps painfully along, his feet twisted almost backward. 'Allah, Allah,' they chant. And above the city, hanging in the heat and dust, echoing their call, from a tall minaret of the mosque comes 'la ilaha illa Allah' ('there is no god but God') calling the faithful to prayer.

Vyasiki has arranged a dinner for me to meet some influential men who've heard I want to help. We sit on mats on the floor with banana leaves in front of us. Vyasiki sprinkles drops of water around the leaf 'to keep the bugs from crawling into your food'. They drink by pouring the water into their mouths without touching the rim of the cup. When I try it, I spill the water all down me, making everyone laugh. 'Never mind,' I say, 'it's very refreshing in this heat.' The food is served, the server dipping his hand into the rice and dropping a handful on the leaf, dahl is ladled on to vegetables. There is no silverware, the Bengalis roll the rice into neat balls and pop them into their mouths. I follow awkwardly using only my right hand, as is the custom, but I'm repulsed by having people's dirty hands in the food, by the pesky flies which settle on a pile of milk sweets we eat for dessert, by the water with its greenish tinge, and by eating with my hands. I remember Animisha's warnings, but I also remember that I have come here to serve. 'Lord,' I

* A popular deity and demi-god who annhilates the material world and supervises the material made of ignorance.

pray, 'this is your programme. If you want this work, protect me.'

The men are talking about a temple that has been donated to the devotees in Sylhet. The moment I hear the name Sylhet I feel an intense rush of emotion, feel faint and dizzy and pleasure all mingled together. I know that Sylhet is the home of the family of Lord Chaitanya, an incarnation of Krishna, in the form of a perfect devotee who appeared in Bengal 500 years ago, but why the word Sylhet should affect me so strongly is a mystery to me.

*   *   *   *

Sweet and sour, city of Dhaka; I can't understand the terrible poverty I see all around me or the sweetness of the people who suffer it. Near Farmgate the car stops for a light. A beggar sits on the kerb like a mongrel dog who sniffs gingerly at the edge of life and gets kicked for his trouble. He retreats humbled, sits licking his wounds, wrapping the stumps of his legs in dirty rags and watching with famished eyes, *life* driving by and hardly noticing him. You were careless, my friend, he thinks to himself. You seem to have mislaid your life and when you weren't looking, they stole it. So now he must beg for a small piece of what is his; a penny from a fortune. Our eyes meet and he starts to crawl towards the car. 'Oh no!' I think. I'm not carrying any money. Neither is Vyasiki. I'm hoping the light will change, but it doesn't. He makes his way slowly towards us and pulls himself up the side of the car. He holds out his hand. Please, his eyes beg. I'm upset that I have no money with me, so I give him a small bag of sweets I'm holding on my lap. I'm sure he'll be disappointed or even angry. I watch as he opens the bag and looking in curiously takes a sweet and puts it into his mouth. He looks over at me and smiles. It radiates towards me brilliant as a thousand suns. There is no smallness in his smile. He places his tired hands together and bows his pathetic head before God. With this gesture he seizes my heart, not only for himself but for all who suffer, seizes it and doesn't let go.

I want to help. Trying to find out how, Vyasiki and I go from office to office. Fans rotate slowly in the government offices, not cooling, but pushing the heat around in sweltering circles and fluttering the edges of mountains of paper pinned to the desks by stone weights and bureaucracy. 'Fill out all these forms,' we are told. Twelve copies each.

The foreign aid people are helpful, very hospitable. They welcome us to their air-conditioned offices, a pleasure after the burning streets, offering us cold drinks, biscuits, tea. They give a great deal of their time, patiently answering questions, giving advice. They show us pictures and charts. I'm given extensive reports to read, in-depth studies compiled at great expense by experts in various fields. But for all the charts and graphs, the glossy pamphlets, I still can't understand why 40,000 children die of hunger, or hunger-related diseases, every single day in the world when there are huge surpluses of food – mountains of butter, milk and grains – destroyed or kept in storage at great expense.

* * * *

Wanting to see as much as possible, we drive down the spine of the country towards the Bay of Bengal to

Pundarik Dham, an ashram in Chittagong.

I'm entranced by the countryside, the flats of acid green paddy, rich brown earth, wholesome as bread, the trees of betel, palm and banana.

We cross rivers of saints and sadhus,* the same rivers that flowed 500 years ago. Flakes of sunlight fall like snow into the waters, blinding the grazing fish.

In a small temple Vyasiki dances with the harmonium around his neck and sings in the heart-rending Baul style:

Sri Krishna Chaitanya, Prabhu Doya koro more
(Sri Krishna Chaitanya, please give your mercy)
Toma Bina ke doyalu jagata samsara?
(Who except You is more kind in this material world?)

Somewhere in the cerebral cortex of my consciousness one more small fine wire of attachment, like a golden hair, snaps, sounding a delicate ping, hardly noticed.

At night lying on a hard wooden bed that makes my bones ache, I hear the jungle machinery surging, clanking, turning on itself, like a great factory.

From my window I can see the trees bend under the weight of the moon and moisture running down their spiral leaves, dripping in great lumps on to the ground.

This country, God-intoxicated, pounds on through fiery days, pounds through the primaeval night, pounds on and on pounding me down to my very essence.

* * * *

* Saintly person, holy man, generally an ascetic.

The sun like a ripe red fruit is slowly swallowed by the earth, turning the pools filled with hyacinth and lotus flowers violet. It's the time when the cows come home from the fields, their bells jangling, kicking up dust clouds of ochre earth which mingle with wood smoke as the women in the village light fires to cook the evening meal. In the distance, across the meadow, a conch is blown to welcome the night.

I'm walking barefoot along the forest path with Nistula, the temple president, returning from a visit to the Bhajan Kutir* of Mukunda Datta. It's a small stone building, little bigger than a man's body. Fallen into disrepair, the stones overgrown with grass, a tree taken root in the dome. I crawl into the tiny space to sit and meditate where the saint, an associate of Lord Chaitanya, had sat 500 years ago in the cool dark, wrapped in his stone shroud, away from distraction, chanting and praying.

Nistula's a natural comic, he's teasing me. 'Rytasha, why aren't you wearing your wellies? Aren't you worried the snakes will get you?'

Terrified I tell him, 'Don't even mention the word snake!'

Out of nowhere a gypsy woman appears on the path. 'Snake?' she says, 'You want snake?'

'No, thank you very much,' I say. 'That's the last thing I want.'

As I speak she takes down the woven basket she is carrying on her head and places it on the ground in front of us. Her bangles jingle as she removes the lid and turns

* A small hut in which a renounced devotee lives, worships and performs devotional service.

the basket upside down depositing a thick tangle of snake inches from my bare feet. The king cobra lies on the ground stunned for a second and then each individual vertebra begins to slowly undulate, one by one, under the scaly skin. Coiling and uncoiling, it lifts its head up and stands in front of us with its hood spread, swaying back and forth, its cold reptilian eye watching, waiting to strike. The woman plays with it, tapping it, teasing it till hissing, it strikes at her, but she is always too fast for it. I watch, petrified, not daring to move a muscle.

'Bakshish?[*]' she asks, holding out her hand. 'An offer one can hardly refuse,' I say to Nistula as we give her some *taka*.[†]

* * * *

My last night in Bangladesh promises a storm. In my room at the temple I'm lying on my bed reading Jaiva Dharma, while outside in a tamarind tree a pair of Hekel Jekel crows scream at each other belligerently on a branch above the Bramacaris who are loading a truck with books and tapes to sell at a *mela*[‡] on the Brahma Putra river later that night.

They've invited me to go. 'Heavy programme,' says Nitai Mantra, 'many many people, maybe 100,000.' Everyone will stay up through the night listening to different gurus and sadhus preaching, listening to *kirtan* and *bhajan*[§] and watching the *jatra* plays. At sunrise they will go to bathe in the Brahma Putra, washing away

* Alms.
† Bangladesh money.
‡ Fair.
§ Devotional songs praising the Lord.

their sins.

The wind has picked up rolling miles of billowing purple clouds towards the city and besides I'm fascinated by my book. No, I'll stay here I decide, settling in cosily for the night, but an insistent voice keeps hammering in my head and won't let me concentrate. 'Go!' it says.

The first thing I see when I get out of the truck is a fenced-off enclosure with a crowd of people standing around looking in. I peek over the top of their heads to see inside a group of naked men wearing nothing but heavy iron chains and locks, imprisoning their bodies, symbolizing the incarceration of the soul in the material body. They leave their bodies filthy with neglect, their hair hangs in long dirty rolls, their narcotic eyes glazed and horrible, they beat on drums and bang at metal gongs creating a hellish din. They gallop around the enclosure carrying an older man on their shoulders. Narul, leader of a Muslim sect.

Nitai Mantra pulls me away. 'Come, Mataji,' he says and leads me to a small tent where the boys are sitting.

In the soft golden shadow of a kerosene lamp I sit in the back talking with Nitai looking at the young Bengali boys their sweet faces close together as they study *shastra*;[*] one boy, his arm around another's shoulder in a brotherly gesture.

'Look,' Nitai says, pointing to the opening of the tent. I lean forward and see a slim figure standing in the doorway, his face hidden in the shadows. I feel myself falling into a swoon, feel faint and dizzy and pleasure all min-

* Scripture, sacred teaching or treatise.

gled together, as I did when I first heard the word Sylhet. He bends down to enter and I am able to see his face for the first time. It takes my breath away, it is so beautiful. 'He's a caste *goswami** from Sylhet, from the Misra family. A direct descendant of Lord Chaitanya,' Nitai explains.

He stands in the doorway, like a messenger, oblivious of his beauty and more beautiful because of it, beckoning to me. I get up and follow him, out into the night, protected on either side by his followers who clear a path for us through the *mela*.

Night of light. Light from the kerosene lamps' flickering tongues that lick greedily at display counters of gleaming glass bangles, cosmetics, kohl and henna, essential oils, attar of roses, musk and patchouli, mounds of pungent spices, boxes of combs, vials of Ayur-Vedic† medicines curing everything from snake bite to impotence. The flames lick hungrily at the *jalabe* sweets that fry in great vats of bubbling oil, twirling in tubs of hot saffron-scented syrup, in the makeshift shops that line the river bank.

Light burns passionately in the ghee lamps offered to the goddess Kali. Riding a lion, a gift from her father, Himalaya, king of the mountains, she wears a necklace of bony skulls and in her long black hair lies death. Garish with blood greed, she turns her butchering weapons in the ten directions of space.

Light flares and fuses under the *pandals*‡ attracting

* Member of a priestly family who assume the status of goswami by birthright.
† System of medicine based on the Vedas.
‡ Large outdoor tent.

insects and followers in equal amounts. They sit by the thousand wrapped in *chadars*, with sleeping children listening for hours to an assortment of gurus and sadhus in world-worn saffron; to puffed-up philosophers wearing *kurtas** starched with arrogance and theory; to various charismatic charlatans several of whom claim to be God.

They enjoy the kirtaneers, the wandering minstrels, the Bauls, rock stars of Bengal with long hair and sashes tied around their waists who sing seductively to God and play fiddles with carved birds' heads, drums, and the *ectara*, a one-stringed instrument; disturbing the ocean of love of God with their hysterical dramas of sweet-salt tears.

We stop to watch the Jagai Madai play. Lord Nityananda, the brother of Lord Chaitanya, preaching to the drunkards Jagai and Madai who are so intoxicated they cannot hear. Their ears only use is to hang earrings on. Angry as the ignorant often are, they throw a wine pot hitting Lord Nityananda and cutting his forehead. Struck he falls, slowly, almost tenderly. Tumbling out of time. He falls to rise, falling not from grace but to grace.

A shadow passes over the moon, unseen, and suddenly I'm standing beside my bones. All the night contains is now seen transparent, God in everything and everything in God, yet He stands apart so that love may exist.

From far away a voice says, 'Ashen – come.' I realize that I am chanting, that my beads are in my hands as I follow the young *goswami* through the *mela*. Wherever

* Long loose shirt, usually worn by Indian men.

we go we are greeted and asked to sit, garlanded, offered refreshment, but we don't stay anywhere.

We walk miles to the end of the *mela*, to a massive banyan tree hundreds of years old, where the Shaivites, followers of Lord Siva, are found. Wearing red loincloths, carrying tridents, their foreheads marked with three streaks of ash, they camp under the sheltering tree, smoking ganja.[*]

We are led to a small white temple, to the potent black stone Siva Lingam.[†] The *pujari* comes forward carrying a metal bowl filled with fruit, which has been offered to Lord Siva. In the bowl a large black beetle crawls under chunks of mango, watermelon and papaya.

Through the long night I chant and remember and soon the holy names begin to chant me and with every syllable I wake up, becoming more and more awake, as though living I had slept, by dreaming I had endured; till the sun rises in the cloud banks across the river watched by a weakening moon and the multitudes of people move up and down the steps to the bathing *ghat*,[‡] pressing and pushing towards the cleansing water. To escape the crowds some rent the little bark boats that dot the water and bathe off them in the centre of the large calm river. The devotees join us, pleased that they have had a profitable night selling books and tapes and posters. Together we go down the slippery stone steps, buoyed on a wave of people, to put our feet in the river and sprinkle water over ourselves and each other. The

* Marijuana
† A worshipful symbol of Lord Siva
‡ Bathing place along a river bank, with stone steps descending into the water.

river, conscious and unconscious, flows by full of sin.

Because this day is auspicious and the pilgrims will be generous, many beggars have lined the path leading away from the river, each allotted a piece of ground to lie his piteous body on. Like merchants, they exhibit their wares, selling their diseases and disorders, showing the horrifying extent of the cruelty the body can exact on man.

They wave rotting stumps smelling sickeningly of gangrene; they look at you out of empty eye sockets oozing pus; show their bodies covered head to foot in boils. Freakish afflictions abound, a man with a pointed head the size of an orange has brought his friend, a torso with a head, on a wooden plank with little wheels, which he has pulled here from the outskirts of the city, hoping to earn some *taka*.

'Oh God, why?' I say, but I know why. In leaving God it is we who curse ourselves, by our own action.

Lifetime after lifetime we earn ourselves, our bodies created by our consciousness. We build our world brick by brick, action by action. Every moment of anxiety we have earned, every holocaust we have obtained by our own effort.

As we walk slowly together towards the time of leaving, I study the face of the *goswami*, an old man's face brittle with age and wisdom, but then he turns to me to say goodbye and I'm looking into the eyes of a fresh-faced boy, barely nineteen, who is smiling at me.

Suddenly he is gone. I stand on the dusty path, oblivious to my surroundings, calling to God, remembering my vision, in a reality beyond thought. 'Oh Lord,' I pray, 'You have wounded me, and from these wounds all my life is flowing, all past and future, all codes, beliefs and ideas; with a single blow all appearance and illusion. Wound me again, that I may finally die of You.'

CHAPTER 10

I put on the white dress of death, white of widows and renunciates. I put on the white of the wedding, white of the spiritual marriage; a white with no domesticity stitched into the fabric. I long to see Srila Gurudeva, as a child longs for his mother. I want to lay myself down at his feet, swimming in the ocean of his mercy, I am too narrow to contain.

I write him a letter; inept. To speak of my experience is beyond me, to put it into words impossible. To put the spiritual into the material is like trying to describe colour to the blind, music to the deaf.

The letter causes an uproar among the leaders. 'How does she think she can have an experience even the spiritual master hasn't had?' says Maharaja. My programmes are stopped, I'm preached against in the temple. They call in my son and forbid him to speak to me, to associate with me. They interrogate me for hours. One man asks, 'So now you think you're so advanced, you can have this kind of experience.'

'Oh, no,' I stammer horrified. 'Surely . . . it's cause-
less mercy. It's precisely because I'm not advanced . . .'

'No!' he shouts, slamming his fist on the table.
They're losing patience with me. 'It's not possible for a
neophyte to have this experience.'

'But what about St Paul? He was even persecuting the
Christians and . . .'

'That religion is completely bogus.'

When I hear this I stop arguing. I hold my anger in my
mouth, swallow my unspoken words. This isn't spiritual-
ity, it's fanaticism. So I stop, but they go on and on, roll
on and on, grinding me down, torturing me with their
accusations.

'You're selfish! You've never loved Seila Gurudeva.
He gave you everything. You're incapable of love.'

'No!' I cry.

Gurudeva is sitting on the *vyasasan*, his face like
stone. 'This is happening because of your independence,
because you've not surrendered to me, because you insist on associating with my enemies.'

'Enemies?'

'Vyasiki for one.'

'Oh, no, Srila Gurudeva. He's never said anything
against you.'

'Not only him,' he continues, 'there are others. The
trouble with you, Rytasha, is that you still trust your
mind. You must forget everything that's happened and
just surrender to me,' he says running his hand sen-
suously up and down the rich silk of the *vyasasan*.
'Rytasha, you cannot jump over me to go to Krishna.'

This is the culmination of so many things I didn't want

to look at. Now I'm forced to watch as Religion pulls up its robes; exposing itself; showing the obscene genitals of power politics.

'Come,' says Animisha, 'we're leaving,' and we do. 'We're not going back,' he says. There's a finality in his voice I've never heard before.

* * * *

Something fierce, ugly, grows in my heart; I hate them for making me hate them. I hate them because I had loved them, still love them. Though I know I can't serve, can't progress – I don't think even God wants me to stay – I still can't help longing for the early innocent days of Srila Prabhupada.

'Certainly, not all organization has to be bad. Look at the church,' I say to Animisha, 'it's produced many great saints.'

'They've become saints in spite of the church,' he argues.

I can never exhaust my anger, polishing it till it shines by going over and over again every injustice, every betrayal of spiritual principle, of moral principle, trying to understand how religion can block the religious ex-perience. I polish it till it glares with a white heat that shines back on to myself. 'Maybe they're right,' I say to Jamuna. 'Maybe I need to be humbled, humiliated.'

'No, Rytasha. You don't learn humility by being humiliated. You learn humility by being with people who are humble.'

I'm swamped by despair: in my room, in my bed, my hair is full of it. I doubt everything and everyone. Even the stars that no longer exist, burnt out millions of years ago, appear to shine.

We still have to finish the film. I can't face it. 'You must,' Anna says. 'You're a bridge between two worlds.' One I haven't crossed myself, I think.

So we film. 'Yes,' I say, 'I have to leave. I want to live by everything he represents, but I have to leave.' It practically breaks my teeth those final words, but I know only the truth ever works. If I'm going to be damned, I may as well be damned by the truth.

When the film comes out, Srila Gurudeva is furious. He tells Anna, 'Rytasha has committed spiritual suicide and you've given her the knife.' I want him to forgive me, even if I can't go back to him, but he won't see me. 'She's made her bed, let her lie in it,' is his comment.

The film is a huge critical and artistic success. Anna wins the Kodak award, an award created especially for her as the 'Best Young Director' of 1986. We're invited to a luncheon in her honour at the National Film Theatre where excerpts from the film are shown and Maria Aitken presents her with the award for *Persuaders*. 'I like the young part,' says Anna.

Channel Four is flooded with mail, more than any other programme they have shown. I receive hundreds of sympathetic letters.

To Srila Gurudeva I'm an outlaw, a Judas whose kiss leaves an aftermath of betrayal. Though threatened with death, the void, an excess of wounds, I'm more threatened by my praise, by the lie of my prodigal return to the world.

I have killed the king and the land lies barren. Being exiled I am forced to cross many frontiers. I call and call. No one takes my hand. No one hears my call. My prayers howl like ferocious animals. They come back hungry.

My mother says, 'I knew what he was when I saw those ostentatious rooms of his, that black marble bathroom with the gold taps. He was living more like a king than a holy man.'

I meet Roman O'Reilly on the Kings Road. 'Good for you,' he says. 'You really nailed that guy.'

'I did not "nail him",' I say, offended.

'Man, I wouldn't have touched him with a ten-foot pole. The arrogance of the guy was unbelievable.'

I walk away, tears stinging my eyes.

Since the film, the house is full of people who put their feet in the door like salesmen, each trying to get me to buy the same commodity: conversion. Every religion has been represented, has sat like mirror images on the sofa, saying the same thing: that theirs is the way, the only way; that they are the chosen people; that theirs is the most complete; the last; the best; the final; but I no longer wish to belong to any group over another, for though they all preach brotherhood, all organized beliefs are based on the separation of brother from brother. For the rest of my life I only want to belong to God, to be the humble servant of all God's servants.

* * * *

In 1985, I set up Food Relief International, a non-sectarian, non-political, non-profit making organization dedicated to helping those in disasters or disastrous conditions.

Returning to Bangladesh, I begin immediately to work, doing my first food programme for a Dhaka orphanage that's in an emergency, having lost their Canadian funding and with no money to feed the children until their new sponsorship arrives.

Located in the old part of the city, it had been a grand white wedding cake of a building when it was founded by a group of philanthropic Hindu gentlemen at the turn of the century, but the tropics, time and neglect have turned it into a splendid decrepit old wreck, a Miss Haversham of a house, now home and family for one hundred little orphans.

The old woman who runs the orphanage holds a stub of a pencil above a row of figures. Concentrating she screws her mouth up into a network of wrinkles. Her long grey hair hangs in oily strings down her broad back, absentmindedly she twists it into a knot at the back of her neck and continues making a list of the food that's needed. 'Rice, dhal, vegetables, powdered milk, sugar.'

'Some fruit,' I suggest.

'Wheat, fish.'

'No,' I say. 'Food Relief International is a vegetarian programme; also I ask that we remember that this food is *prasadam*, the mercy of God and, as you are Hindus, that we offer it to Krishna.'

The fan in the office isn't working and sweat trickles down my body inside my sari. I hope she isn't disappointed or offended, but she smiles at me and says *aacha.*[*]

On the peeling wall, to the right of several electric lines, a lizard slips out from behind a poster of Gaura Nitai, 'tik, tik', he agrees before scurrying under a photo

* Slang Indian word meaning agreement or affirmative.

of the plump Nazrul, the village poet of Bangladesh.

I ladle the lunch on to the metal plates of the children who sit on the floor in long rows in the shade of the verandah. They bend over their plates, eating quickly, with concentrated attention till the rice swells up their bellies and they feel solid and safe. My little brothers and sisters, my children.

* * * *

'Have another pastry, Father.' I say. The Chinese teapot with its designs in turquoise and gold hovers over a plate of strawberry tarts. With his snow-white hair and kindly face, good Father Tracey of the Society of Jesus looks exactly as I imagined God would look when I was a child. 'More tea? It's jasmine. You must be frozen.'

It's a frosty London day and Father Tracey has come all the way from his Farm Street Church. 'So, Father,' I continue, getting back to our discussion, 'the problem for me is that I wonder if I'm really doing service for God. I get so much pleasure out of my work in Bangladesh; I was so happy feeding the children that I wonder about my own motives.'

'Rytasha,' he says, 'you make a serious mistake, condemned by the Church, in thinking that God's work must be unpleasant; actually you can't serve God without getting pleasure yourself.'

'I guess I sort of feel,' I say, 'it's like the old thing about medicine; if it doesn't taste bitter, I wonder if it's doing any good.'

But the bitter comes soon enough. On a clear white night of iced window panes, during a snowstorm of insomnia, it sneaks in like a thief. While the tired city sleeps, gently breathing in and out, in houses with hallways, it insists.

What harsh voices the angels have, not allowing me to sleep out my piece of drowsy dream, to go my own slow way to God.

I shiver in the kitchen at seven past two in the morning, hearing my mind argue with my instincts, which are always right, hearing the order to 'sell everything so that you may give to the poor'.

'Choose,' says the angel's antiseptic voice inside my head. 'God or yourself? Who will you serve?'

'Both,' says the voice of the adulterer in me. The woman in me wants, has needs. 'How will I live with no home, no nest; a woman with no womb? I need my closets with my clothes, freshly pressed, hanging neatly. I need my drawers that smell like cedar to store the documents of my life. I need my shopping, my titles, my designations. Not now. Not yet. Next lifetime. Later! I'm not that strong or pure, or renounced, that I could live with one small trunk filled with nostalgia and a suitcase for travelling.'

But I do. It's all arranged so quickly. In twelve days the flat is sold, the contents, jewellery, books, china, clothing, all sold.

I walk away.

*   *   *   *

A million miles away from Bangladesh, in another world, my mother and I are lunching at the Colony in Palm Beach, sipping designer water between bites of a delicately herbed goats' cheese wrapped in vine leaves.

The waiter grates away with grand ceremony an over-sized wooden pepper shaker, the coarse black grains sprinkling my mother's creamy Pasta Alfredo. I watch impatiently, nibbling a radish that has been pains-takingly carved into a rose.

We are seated by the window, looking out on the bright blue swimming pool at the multicoloured umbrel-las, the men fast-talking business into cordless phones as they bronze in the sun, the women who wear high heels with their bathing suits. At the inside bar several men in pastel sports coats sit nursing stiff drinks.

There is a steady flow of people to our table. 'Hello, Baroness!' they coo. 'Hello, darling!' my mother says. Kisses are exchanged, jewellery rattled. 'Who the hell was that?' my mother asks me.

I'm here on a mission. My mother has raised millions of dollars for different charities. Our library is awash with plaques and statues given in recognition of her work. She has put on fashion shows, run balls, teas and galas. 'I was thinking we could do a ball,' I say. It will have to be something very special to tempt the jaded palate of Palm Beach, where during the season there are as many as two or three events every night. 'It must be glamorous,' says my mother. 'And it should be fun,' I say.

We decide to do a 'send up' of a ball. We invent a mythical Maharaja who invites people to come to a gala where he will pick his one hundredth wife from the assembled guests. We call it 'The Fantasy Ball'. HRH Princess Elizabeth of Yugoslavia is our honorary chair-man. Helen Turner acts as our press agent, getting articles in all the newspapers and magazines, arranging radio interviews and TV coverage. I even appear on the news. The press is fascinated by my riches to rags story and favourable to the charity.

When the invitations go out, they create a furore. The *Miami Post* even runs a satirical commentary on the Maharaja. We're invited everywhere; teas and luncheons are given in our honour. We speak tirelessly about FRI, attracting some wonderful people who sincerely care and wish to help and others who believe that charity begins at home – theirs!

At one such luncheon at the exclusive Governor's Club, in the glass dining room with its stupendous view, a society dowager, not to be outdone in the game of oneupmanship leans over and says to my mother *sotto voce*, 'Of course, I also know the Maharaja. Actually I know his brother better.' My mother and I study our plates intently, not daring to look at each other for fear of laughing in her face.

* * * *

'Once upon a time, in a far-off land, a handsome Prince . . . ' begins the fairy tale; and the Fantasy Ball, as the guests arrive to find what was a ballroom has been transformed, as if by magic, into the rich oriental opulence of a Maharaja's palace by Edward Wignall, FRI's artistic director.

Ed is also the Maharaja. Bedazzling in cloth of gold, bejewelled in barbaric rubies the size of gulls' eggs, ropes of cabachon-smooth sapphires and weighed down by half a ton of Max Factor suntan make-up, he lolls in deeply voluptuous pillows, on leopard skin, under a canopied throne. Saronged attendants, with turbans sprouting exotic ostrich plumes, sit adoringly at his feet and two stand guard fanning him with gigantic rhinestone-encrusted peacock-feather fans.

The air is filled with the sweet smell of success, the spicy aroma of money as Palm Beach tycoonery is whirled around the dance floor.

Imperiously, the Maharaja claps his manicured hands twice and the show begins. Floodlights blaze on to the runways and the orchestra picks up the beat, as top models, each more gorgeous than the other, parade in couture gowns by Countess Alexander of Worth Avenue. They pretend to be interested in becoming the Maharaja's one hundredth wife by flirting outrageously; one even sits herself briefly on his lap, delighting the audience. He pretends to be bored with them. Oh well, after ninety-nine wives!

Dennie Du Boff, who owns North American Kennels and is on the board of FRI, has given a racing greyhound to be raffled and a large Indian silk painting is also donated by Jean-Paul, who is now in the import-export business and has flown in to lend support.

The painting is won by the prominent attorney Christian Searcy, who announces generously that he wants it to be auctioned to the highest bidder to make more money for FRI.

Mark Martin is galvanized into action as master of ceremonies jumps it into high gear and soon has people calling from all over the room till it goes to the highest bidder, my friend Mary Weir.

I speak briefly, nerve-racked, thanking everyone. My mother, as chairman, gets up too. 'Now you can all go home!' she says.

* * * *

By 1987 Gurudeva is no longer a guru; he has left, fallen in disgrace, run off with a woman. Maharaja is gone, too; given up *sanyasa* and married. ISKCON is in schism, a feeding frenzy of icon smashing.

This news doesn't make me happy, being right is no consolation. I feel more alone than ever. The Emperor has no clothes I had said and now, later, they listen, and Anna's film becomes required viewing for all leaders in ISKCON. But for all their faults they were extraordinary men, gold buried in dirt, diamonds in coal, through the guru: God.

According to an unknown plan I had left at the right time, but the leaving hadn't stopped the learning, the lessons weren't over, would never be over. Only the teachers seemed to change but the Teacher remained the same.

CHAPTER 11

With a further half turn of the wheel the heat squeezes what little air is left out of the night. Even at 10 pm it is so stifling I can hardly breathe.

I have to lie down on the massive, ornately carved marriage bed that so far has produced four daughters and unfortunately no sons, in Mr Madana Mohan Saha's house, above his sari shop in Naopara Town, Jessore, as I listen to the local leaders discussing the damage we had seen in the afternoon.

It is a tragedy that our boat, pulled on an undertow of despair, could sail submerged fields and see, deep down below, the rice harvest swaying under the unaccustomed weight of water, drowned by the floods. Eighty per cent of the houses have been destroyed, the crops ruined, leaving the people destitute with nothing to eat and trapped on high ground.

Mr Saha's wife comes in shyly with some Ovaltine, her curious daughter clinging to the tail of her sari. We work out the details of organizing an emergency food distribution programme. We'll need to rent a lorry to get the foodstuff from the markets, and then boats for the last part of the journey as everything is under water.

At daybreak we go to rent a lorry. When I try to pay, the owner stops me. 'No', he says, 'take the truck, a gift. Just pay the petrol.' He doesn't want to make a profit out of the distress of others.

The men climb into the back and I swing up into the high cabin between Mr Saha and the driver to travel to the market at Khulna. After hours of bargaining, buying, loading and unloading we are finally almost at our destination, Ransara village, travelling in a caravan of small boats loaded down low in the water with supplies.

As we approach the village I see acres of people, a whole city of people waiting on the bank. When our boats come into view, a cheer goes up that can be heard echoing across the water like a roar.

Climbing up the slippery bank I am enveloped by the crowd, hands reach out to touch me, Mataji[*], Mataji they call; an old woman throws herself into my arms in tears. The crowd presses in till I can hardly walk. The heat of the sun and thousands of bodies suffocate me, making me feel faint. With our men clearing a path I slowly make my way to a large banyan tree.

The men, 150 local volunteers, unload the boats, set up the *pandals* against the sun and organize the crowds. They dig deep holes in the earth, large enough to stock with firewood, building a long trench of underground ovens. In oil drums with the tops cut off, they cook up a

* Mother, honorary term, showing respect.

hearty *kiteri*; stirring the golden mixture of rice, dahl, vegetables and spice with paddles the size of oars.

So many, too many, too much. They sit patiently waiting as, bent double, I make my way up and down the rows ladling out the *kiteri* to old ladies with collapsed faces, their saris like winding sheets wrapping arms and legs thin as needles; to mothers whose anguish trembles inside their lips, holding damaged babies who lie in their arms, their faces opaque with sleep; to children bowed down beneath a vulnerable neck; and to fathers who must be men. I will give everything but I will never give enough.

Hour after hour, day after day, we work on. People leave and new ones take their place. Before we finish we will have served 25,000 plates of *kiteri*. The heat is relentless. The humidity causes a boil on my back to burst, the pus and blood oozing in my shirt. My feet are burning with dozens of peppery blisters from the red ants and my bones ache from bending over. Feeling my hand stinging like salt I look down to see after hours and hours of work that the weight of the long-handled spoon has cut through my skin and exposed a slice of raw pink flesh. 'Take rest, Mataji,' insists one of the boys.

I retire to the house gratefully, but there is no rest. A new pain afflicts me, greater than any the body can impose. An explosion of despair, dark and black it threatens to swallow me up, annihilate me. I have no energy to fight back. My prayer beads lie mute, entangling my fingers. Unable to pray or even call God's name, I can only listen, hearing my own sobbing, as tears mingled with sweat run down my grimy face. Having no place to bathe, I sit in my filthy clothes spattered with food and stains, the hem black from dragging it in the mud. I'm nauseated by the greasy yellow smell of myself. I long for everything that is clean, holy and kind; for cool white sheets and ice water.

In the temple room next door Mr Saha's ancient grandmother is doing *puja**, ringing a little brass bell at her deities.

I try to move away from my pain by walking around the quiet house. I look into darkened rooms where ghosts of mosquito netting haunt empty beds, round down the stairs to the kitchen with its inventory of pots and pans. Something makes me look up. High up in the corner of the wall a fat hairy brown spider, big as my fist, mucous hanging from her swollen belly is giving birth. Hundreds of tiny spiders are coming out and rushing around the kitchen.

Panic sends me running up the stairs, up and up all the way to the top of the house and out on to the flat roof overlooking the town. I run smack into the blinding bright glare of daylight. Just below to the right are the market alleyways, where a mangy yellow dog pushes his nose in a pile of decaying garbage. At my back flows the river beneath groves of mango and dates, carrying islands of tangled grasses, a flotilla of lilies in its swift currents.

There is a river and there is a door. I don't know how long I watch the rolling water, searching in its horizontal folds till it breaks upon the bank and gives up its secret saying:

---

* Ceremonial worship involving the presentation of offerings to the deities.

'I am the river of life, changing and unchanging . . .
I am the water that Christ walked upon in the Sea of
Galilee, when he bent the universe into miracles
. . .
I am the water that lapped at the banks of the Saras-
vati 5,000 years ago when Narada Muni sang the
supreme Lord Krishna into the Vedas of Vyas . . . I
am the water that Mohammed dreamed in the
desert . . . The sea that Moses parted . . . Holy
water of the word, the water of acts, that cools the
hot eye, blesses the mind, soothes the troubled
heart . . . the only cure for the world.'

When there is nothing more to hear I still continue to
look into the water till it grows black and phosphorous
and the moon's thin incision cuts into the face of night.

The men have waited patiently respecting my medita-
tions. 'Is there any way we can control these horrible
floods?' I ask. Sadly there is not; at least not on the scale
that I could work, perhaps governments . . . but there is
something that can be done.

'Mataji, if we could grow crops in the dry season, we
could store or sell it, then if the floods come, it isn't as
bad; but it will need deep tube wells to bring the water
to the surface and electricity to run them; much money.'

Though we're all tired, I'm anxious to hear so we discuss costings of the machinery, running in the electric
lines from Poli Bidut; how much, how many. Mr Saha
says, 'It will generate possibly 365,000 meals a year feeding 1,000 people.'

'OK. Let's do it!'

*   *   *   *

The early morning in Dhaka is still pleasantly fresh. It leans cool green elbows on the kitchen windowsill of the large house, locked securely behind high gates, quietly, so as not to disturb the family still asleep in various bedrooms or the portly gentleman with corrugated grey hair as he bends to fix breakfast for the little marmalade cat, Miki.

Anisul Islam, grandson of a Muslim saint, grandfather to many grandchildren, an extensive family man, is my guardian angel and protector in Bangladesh. President of the Bangladesh Survey Organization he's responsible for all the maps of the country and more. Author, philosopher, reciter of the Ramayan and Koran, philanthropist, head of the Rotary and a whole roster of organizations; he's a leading member in good standing with the anti-red tape brigade; men who can pick up a phone and with a few words get things done that can't be done. Working together with the Rotary, in July of 1987 when 70 per cent of the country is devastated by floods, Food Relief International supplies seeds for wheat, mustard and rice to the farmers, house-repairing materials, thread to the weavers and large quantities of food grains.

It's early yet. There's still time to work on the short story he's writing before Ishmael, his driver, comes to take him to his office, where I'm waiting.

He comes through the door with a big 'hello', beaming in delight at seeing me, Ishmael right behind with his briefcase. He takes my hands in a warm grasp, asking, 'Have you come alone? I could have sent my car. Have you eaten? A cold drink? When did you arrive?' 'And you?' I ask. 'Yes, yes, I'm pulling on.'

As usual he's doing ten things at once, speaking on the phone to a government minister, looking over the survey work the clerks bring for him to check from the studio next door, arranging for his granddaughter to be picked up at school.

'If so? How so?' I want to know. Together we are building a school in the Kilgoan slums, bringing in water and electricity, constructing an outdoor kitchen where 164 children will be fed nourishing meals, will learn to read and write English and Bengali on a two-year course including maths, geography, history, physical education, and hygiene.

Very quickly it has become obvious that any real change will never happen without education, the gravity of ignorance is too strong. Man's conditions will never change unless man is changed.

Beast, the slums of Kilgoan, encampments of the wretched who live miserable lives jammed together in fragments of shacks, piled up on each other with no sanitation; where during the rainy season the urine and faeces boiling in the open drains mixes in the drinking and bathing water. Here, young children work long hours breaking stones or roaming the city streets collecting bits of paper, scraps of metal to sell. These are our children.

We are working with Provati Sangshad, a group of dedicated young men, mostly college students, who give their time freely, teaching the children and helping the project. 'The meals must be vegetarian,' I am telling the boys, 'and, as you are Muslim, we must pray to Allah.'

'Remember, Rytasha,' Mr Islam jokes, his soft brown eyes thoughtful behind his glasses, 'no good deed goes unpunished!'

The dealings are difficult and there is much work, a mountain of work, lifetimes of the stuff. There is the heavy realization that there are forces of vested interest with not the slightest flicker, not even a little conscience, who foster superstition, division, the repetitive ignorance; and on purpose!

If anyone were to ask me who had made the countries, divided up the world, building borders that lock their brothers out and who had taken God's word dividing it up, using religions to separate man from man, I would answer that there are no boundaries, no borders in this world or in the next except those made by man.

But it is not yet the time. It is the time to work, to learn, to go back to the West, and raise the money.

Like the Monks of Krak de Chevaliers, who putting armour over their black robes rode out from their brutal fortress monastery to do battle in the crusades, I travel back and forth between East and West, England and America.

*　*　*　*

On fixed dates, at specific hours, the Fantasy Ball ignites a kaleidescope of celadone, mica, quartz and colour; of perfumes and bare shoulders balancing sacrificial breasts on fashion plates. Our first event in London is organized by Chairman Sally Farmiloe, with honorary patrons Margaret, Duchess of Argyll and The Princess Helena Montafian MBE, and as President, the Countess of Burford. Hazel O'Connor sings in cabaret, there is a fashion show by Enrico Coveri, and Bill Wyman of the Rolling Stones presents the prizes.

60 Minutes comes to film and goes back with me to Bangladesh, making 'The Angel of Bengal'.

* * * *

Channel Four approaches Anna. 'Whatever became of Rytasha?' they ask. When Anna tells them they ask us to do a sequel to *Persuaders*. So at our next Fantasy Ball, when Father Tracey leans across the table and asks Cynthia Payne, the most notorious Madame in London, 'And what do you do, my dear?', Anna is there to film it.

She also comes to Palm Beach. The blonde leading the blind. 'Step into my office, Rytasha,' Anna says grandly, as she ushers me into the tiny bathroom. 'What, what, what?' she says, her hands fluttering up and down. 'What?' I say as if I didn't know.

We're filming a committee meeting at my mother's. The blinds have been drawn in the room. On the white Savonarie rugs pastel roses bloom as the Louis Quinze chairs wrap themselves around the members who are busy balancing cups and cake as they indulge in ego-petting, giving lessons on dressing for fashion victims; every hair in place, every feeling repressed, chit-chatting for the camera.

From her seat on the toilet, Anna looks up at me. I know that look. 'Give me a break, Rytasha. This is so boring and so phoney.' Cunning as a cat with a sixth sense, she has quickly found out all about the frictions and factions and 'I want you to bring them out, open it up,' she says.

'If I do that we won't have a committee,' I plead.

'I want to show the struggle,' she continues, 'not only in Bangladesh but here also, show the reality of fund-raising, how difficult it is to work with a group of strong-minded people, each feeling they're right, pulling in different directions.' She's on a roll now and she's right. 'I don't want to show them in a bad light. I want to show how much they care and how willing they are to fight for it, a little of the passion we know is there.' Do we ever!

My heart is beating me up, as I begin addressing the meeting. 'There are some problems I think we should talk about,' and then watch as all hell breaks loose.

Later my mother does an interview, seated at her Venetian-glass dressing table in an ecru lace peignoir, going rather heavy on the diamonds, and saying, 'Of course I'm very proud of Rytasha, but like any mother I would like to see her married, and when I say married, I mean money!'

* * * *

The sun crackles against the noon sky and dust casts a fine sepia mist over the scenery as our train chugs slowly through the countryside from Dhaka to Chittagong, its fans sponging up what's left of the air, the windows wide open to the scorching heat. Waiters in dirty white jackets, left over from the Raj go up and down the aisles with tea and plates of food with thick slices of bread and cutlets and chutney. The men wipe their faces and hands on their handkerchiefs.

Outside the flat land crumples into peaks as we reach the hill tracts of Chittagong where I'm bound to discuss building a school in Ramsara with Nistula.

Climbing down from the train after the weary hours, I find the station square deserted; no baby taxis, no rickshaws, no nothing, only a convoy of army trucks bristling at the entrance to the city. Going over to an official-looking army officer, I ask him what's happening. 'Hartal strike.' Another of the many strikes that bring the country to a standstill on a regular basis, the people's only voice against the government. 'But I have to get to Hatazari,' I say. 'The hartal will end by six, then you can go.'

At five minutes to six, after four hours of waiting, one lone baby taxi limps into the square. I make a determined dash for it. I don't want to have to travel through the countryside at night.

I'm negotiating the fare with the driver when we hear shots in the distance, followed by a stampede of men who race through the square, sprinkling it with their blood, chased by the police a few seconds later. Armed with guns and shots, blows and fractures they charge across the square striking down anyone in sight. A policeman runs at me, his baton swung up high above his head. I stand my ground as he approaches. Why should I run? Something makes me smile at him. It stops him dead in his tracks. He smiles back. He's young, looks less than twenty, and then, remembering himself again, he races by me.

When I finally reach Nistula, in the dead of the night, he's amazed to see me. 'How did you get through? The whole city is rioting. They're fighting in the streets.'

As soon as peace is restored we leave for Jessore to begin building a school in Ramsara. After the first meeting with the local leaders, Nistula comes over to me. 'Ah . . . Rytasha . . . the men say you shouldn't go to the brickyards to buy the bricks. They said to tell you that in this country women don't go to the brickyards.' 'Well, you tell them,' I say, 'that in this country women don't build schools either.'

When the school is built and running the government cites it in a report as the best school in the district and gives one of our boys a scholarship. By 1988, we have opened up another ten schools taking over 1,000 children, the poorest of the poor, who otherwise would have had no opportunity for any education.

We run camps in Dhaka when the city is flooded, give seed to the farmers and repair houses after a cyclone in Pautakali. Mr Islam and I visit Mymensingh where we put in a much-needed tube well. Before this the people had to walk two miles just to get some clean water.

Because of our work, I'm very honoured to be invited to a Rotary meeting, the enclave of the most powerful men in Bangladesh. I'm seated on the dais, which surprises me, and I am even more surprised, and dismayed, when I hear them announce that the guest speaker for the night is . . . me!

* * * *

I meet many sadhus, gurus and holy men, one 114 years old. This guru is the oldest man I've ever seen, his ancient eyes clouded grey, blindfolded by film, a tube coming out of his body, the bottle on the end held by his doctor who sits right behind him. I can feel the warmth of the love of his disciples who fill the room, sitting on the floor at his feet. He gestures for me to sit next to him on the wooden platform. His shrunken mouth moves as he tries to speak to me so I lean close to him till I feel his breath whisper to my ear. 'Chant the Holy Names,' it says.

In Rajashi near Prem Toli where we feed 30,000 people, I'm befriended by a young *babaji**, full of the energy of a high spiritual metabolism, an intense austerity, possessing nothing and possessed by nothing. God's holy fool.

I make a pilgrimage to Prem Toli and wade into the river, the cool grey clay oozing between my toes. India to my back, I gaze at the top of the tree, which shimmers like crushed glass in the sky, surrounded by its small temple.

On one brief day out of eternity, under this tree, Lord Chaitanya had given *prema*, pure love of God, and the tree, love-stricken, had blossomed with ripe meteors, with whole constellations, with never-before-seen colours, a new thick white light. Exquisite flowers burned like stars on its branches, which bowed down in reverence as explosions of ecstasy scattered the seeds of the Holy Name which fell to the fertile ground.

A music with the appetites of iron sprouts in my left ear; a banging cacophony of drums and kartals calls me to the temple door. Inside a group of strange women, in garish saris, their turgid chunks of mouths a greasy red, nails and feet stained with henna dance wantonly around the trunk of the sacred tree whose roots shelter the deities.

Members of the notorious sect that mimics the *gopis*, the highest spiritual taste of mystic love, confusing the sexual with the spiritual . . . and they are men!

* Respectful title for a holy man.

CHAPTER 12

My body doesn't appreciate these hectic ramblings, my life spliced together by jet flights, the uneaten meals, the change of water and language, the wretched exhaustion. My health is flopping down around my ankles, my skin loosened and tightened by geography. My scalded lungs cough up a viscous mix, my bowels, a factory of parasites and, worst disease of all, the freezing fevers of a first-rate anxiety.

I run down the airport corridors, 'Just hand luggage,' I say.

Today the sun will come up twice, as the earth tilts up a second sunrise over the braided fields, spiced and curved on the great subcontinent of India. I have my doubts that tons of steel will fly. '*Inshallah*, God willing,' the captain announces. So on take-off I make bargains, selling myself to God again. Ha! as if He needs me and my petty promises and trade-offs.

The captain knows my work and invites me to the

cockpit to talk. First class is empty, so they make up a bed out of the front row of seats where I can take rest.

Rocked in my metal cradle, mile high in the sky among the stars, I sleep, half-waking only when I sense the figure of the captain, kneeling on the floor, saying his prayers. Confused by fatigue and sleep, I don't know where I am. Oh, yes, I remember, I'm here. It's always here. It's always now.

*   *   *   *

Exhausted by the flight, I hardly notice the young man I'm introduced to at the Dhaka temple either. 'You should talk,' I'm told. 'You're both involved in the same work.'

He's got a big position with World Vision, degrees in social work, a great deal of government service behind him and a burning desire to serve his people. I finally wake up fully only when he tells me. 'I love all the saints and prophets of all the religions.' It is extremely rare to find such a broad outlook in sectarian Bangladesh, unusual to meet a Muslim at a Hindu temple. The last thing he says before he leaves is, 'God has sent me to help you.' 'Hmm,' I think.

Razzaque Khan was born in a small village in Rajashi in East Pakistan; given an honourable father, good mother, sisters, brothers, and poverty. When he was twelve, nationwide tests were held to find the most brilliant boys in the country and out of millions, fifty were chosen, sent to cadet college to be trained along with the sons of the elite as the future leaders of the country.

He found himself not only with shoes now, but splendid uniforms, fine food, privilege and education. Only English was allowed at meals. He was an outstanding student, powerful athlete, a natural leader, but there was also a more thoughtful side that asked the questions and drew him towards the centre.

* * * *

On the twenty-fifth of March, 1971 at 11:30 pm Pakistani soldiers stole through the night into the University of Dhaka, into the student halls, into the dormitories where the young boys lay peacefully sleeping. They would never wake up! The morning would find their bodies emptied into their sheets, their faces blurred with blood on their pillows.

Only then did Pakistan declare war.

Glory, Glory, Glory, all glories to war. The glorious victory of millions dead.

When the War of Liberation began, Razzaque Khan was a schoolboy of sixteen living in East Pakistan. Nine months later he was a man and Bangladesh had won its freedom.

He had joined the Freedom Fighters, going across into India to be trained and returning to fight in the barefoot army, ill equipped with everything but courage against the oppressive military machine of Pakistan. He was brave and lucky. A bullet passed through him killing his cousin. In the field men died all around him. The country was burning with atrocities. A plague of blood rained down upon the people.

On the seventh of September, 1971 his luck ran out. Swimming eight miles across the river, he was captured by the Pakistanis at Prem Toli. Secret papers were found on him. They transported him by truck, the soldiers cursing him, kicking him, beating him all the way, till he protested, 'I'm a man like you,' and they stopped; perhaps because there was worse to come or because he had touched them. The torture he experienced under the Pakistanis could still make him cry sixteen years later; could make him cry, but not talk.

They sentenced him, a boy barely sixteen, to death. In the morning he would be executed. They put him in a cell crowded with thirty other condemned men to wait out the time when the night and their lives would end and life's limits might become limitless.

At dawn they would walk out into the fresh morning and dew would be on the grass, like any other day. The earth and air would smell sweet, like any other day. The cock would crow as he did yesterday and would tomorrow, familiar things, noticed now and already missed. The strangeness would be the ordinariness, till the guns exacted their ferocious repetition of death; over and over death; stuttering out death and death and more death and afterwards the dew would burn off the grass, as the sun rose, like any other day.

But before this could happen there appeared a small split on a seam and Razzaque noticed it. A door left un-locked, a guard not in position on the roof and he took his chance. What could he lose now anyway? He jumped and ran and ran, running till it hurt; off the roads with his breath burning him in jagged gasps, and he fell in a field to the ground. The rain streaming over his body was cool and good and he was alive and he would be alive in the morning and he would be alive when all the others in the cell were dead. He would be alive, but not the same way; never again in the same way.

'I died in 1972,' he tells me. 'Now there is only service and the search for God.'

Every night just before sunset we meet and take a rickshaw through the narrow streets of Old Dhaka to the port, in time to watch the sun thundering against the final arc of earth, burning the stone of the city in the waters of the river; to walk down the ramps and stand surrounded by the robust bustle on the docks, the pedlars and porters, the big boats whose shuddering motors muted under the vibrating water back tenderly out of the harbour carrying their cargo of human hearts.

Voyagers who neither arrive nor leave, we abandon the known shore in a small boat. Every night for seven days, Razzaque asks and every night for seven days I answer.

'When Christ stood on the Mount,' I continue from the night before, 'He saw the hunger. Before He spoke, He fed the people and satisfied their bodies which are temporary and then He spoke, feeding their souls which are eternal. We are building schools, clinics, irrigation systems; we distribute food, but unless there is medicine not only for the body but for the spirit, where is the care? Unless the water from the tube wells flows with the spirit we will always thirst; and the food we distribute must be the mercy of God. Good works without God is like taking care of the cage but allowing the bird inside to starve to death.'

The boatman's oar carves little whirlpools deep into the black water. Cupping some water in my hand I go on, 'Spiritual life is like water, it needs a vessel to carry it and that vessel is religion.'

The stars and moon slide about on the waves and as we move farther away from the shore, scraps of city sound are shredded into delicate trinkets that sink tinkling against the silent river bed. 'So . . . There is only one God and different religions are only different ways of looking at Him, seeing the same thing but from different angles of vision. Ultimately all religions must lead to love of God.'

Diving deeper, we venture further and further out. Black sky above black water below, the boatman a silent shadow as we move into the realm of three seen by two.

Razzaque leans forward, his head bowed, his gaze turned inward, his forehead serious; his listening so intense that it draws the absolute truth through me and words bred in base metal become gold, and every word I speak, every syllable becomes a prayer, every sentence an act of devotion; speaking, I kneel before God; worshipping with words I repeatedly pay my obeisance before my Lord. Everything I speak is for Him. Everything I speak is from Him.

'When I was a young boy,' Razzaque tells me, 'I was always searching after God; though after a while I would not go to the mosque, I still searched after God. Lately, I spent a year searching knowledge. Every day I went to the river and sat looking into the water, my family wondering about me, a year looking. I spent myself searching after a teacher, travelling to India; but I knew when I met you that the search was over, that I have found my spiritual master.'

Cutting him off, I continue speaking. 'Spiritual life is not about information, but transformation,' I say, pushing quickly on past this dangerous idea.

*   *   *   *

Bangladesh is in a pitiful state. The war it won is lost every day, the peace is hungry and hope is disappointed.

'I have often wondered why I was spared in "71" Razzaque says. 'Now I can understand.' He quits his job to become director of FRI.

We travel together throughout Bangladesh, going to all our projects, training and working, sharing a common vision. Again and again he asks to become my disciple and gets no answer.

In Ramsara, a Hindu village, Razzaque gets up to speak. In a country torn with violent sectarianism, I'm anxious as to whether they will accept a Muslim. I watch the people listening to him, reading their reactions on their faces. Charismatic, a man of the people, a natural leader, he speaks passionately and they respond to him. His jokes tickle ripples of laughter from the audience. They grow serious as he does. The older men nod their heads in agreement and exchange looks and soon he is forming committees, energetically setting up programmes, singling out leaders.

At a meeting of the two villages, Debe Tola and Fultola, he asks the villagers, 'What do you want?' The people are shy. 'We want whatever you want,' they venture. 'Well,' he begins, mock serious, 'What I want? I like to sleep. I want to take my blanket and go back to bed.' The people catch on quickly. 'It can't be what other people want,' he says. 'You must decide what you want. Then,' he explains, 'we must find out your resources. Then I can train you how to use these resources to achieve your goals and FRI will then help you by giving interest-free loans.'

Riding on a rickety cart miles along the rutted roads we arrive back in Ramsara on a steaming afternoon to be greeted by the whole village and a chorus of children singing songs in shining faces and slicked-back hair.

At the schoolhouse there are long glorifying speeches, flowery as the garlands around our necks. Looking up at the ceiling I study the beams, the cobwebs which weave one corner to another. The school is filthy, I don't think it's been cleaned since we built it.

'Get me a broom,' I say to the man next to me, interrupting the speaker.

'Mataji,' he says, 'I will do it later.'

'No, now,' I insist.

The man hesitates. 'We will take care of it, Mataji.'

'Get me a broom,' I repeat.

When the broom is brought I begin whacking angrily at the ceiling and walls bringing down great balloons of dust. Everyone joins in, scrubbing away with brooms made out of bits of branch, wiping down the desks.

By the time I'm finished, my hair is greyed and granules of dirt coat my face and lodge in the edges of my eyes. My lips are dusty with a grainy pollen and my white cloth has grown a tired sepia stain, but I'm satisfied. The school is clean and it remains clean.

In a meeting the next morning, Narayan raises his hand to speak. His wife, Radha, head of the women's committee pulls the end of her sari over her mouth, her dark eyes cast down at the floor. He complains, 'You gave all the women seed and help with their kitchen gardens, but not the men.'

'Oh, so you are complaining?' I ask. 'Your wife

planted the seeds we gave?'

'Yes,' he answers.

'And carried the water from the well to the house by herself in the hot sun to water the plants?' I ask.

'Yes,' he answers.

'And did all the weeding and caring for them?'

'Yes.'

'And when they had grown she picked them and cooking them, served them to you?'

'Yes.'

'And were they good?' I ask.

'Yes, very good,' he answers.

'And so why are you complaining?'

We all crack into laughter, especially Narayan and Rhadah.

'All right,' I say, 'we will give the men's committee seed for gardens also and we will have a contest between the men and women to see who has the best garden.'

* * * *

Noisy stars are clattering against the freezing sky and I am disjointed with excuses and resistance.

'No!' I tell Razzaque again, 'I don't want to be anyone's spiritual master, don't want the responsibility of disciples. I'm not qualified, too young, a woman, but I will help you find a spiritual master.'

I have a terrible feeling that when I prayed to be God's servant, He took me seriously. 'Dear Lord, have you tamed me, just to put me among wild animals, who lie in ambush within and without, with their sharp zigzag of teeth and ambitious appetites. 'Who,' I ask, 'can take a position of power, rising in men's eyes without suffering vertigo?'

I introduce Razzaque to various gurus: Alpha, Omega and all between. Reality and illusion. Holy man and charlatan. Men who may look 'holy' before they speak, until they speak gargling pebbles of knowledge; word jugglery of arcane acrobatics. Religious businessmen; current breakers. In Faridpur there are at least seven men with large followings who claim to be incarnations of God. 'I'd like to invite them all to meet together to see what would happen,' I joke.

We go to the ashram of Lalan, troubadour saint of Bengal, friend of Tagore, who the Hindus claim as a Hindu saint and the Muslims say is an Islamic saint.

'To follow a particular religion,' I tell Razzaque, as we cross the dry river bed outside Kustia, 'is like digging a well. At a certain depth you will hit water; spiritual water. At that point there is only love of God.'

The ashram is a museum with a gaggle of ganja-soaked devotees who have no knowledge, only a senti-mental attachment to a ghost, who hang around licking at a corpse. It seems a total waste of time till one boy, who is a guest himself, sings *Lalans* songs for us. Sitting on a mat, chiaroscuroed by the late afternoon light, he pushes air through the paper bellows of an ivory-inlaid harmonium, singing in a sweet voice the songs that every Bengali loves, that have seeped into the culture because of their beauty and truth.

Everywhere we go I speak with various gurus and sad-hus, often debating philosophically as is the custom so Razzaque can hear. At a temple in Dhaka I speak with the *pujari*, the head priest, a friendly man with a shaved renunciate's head and warm brown eyes. 'Guru is God,' he says, a common misconception in the East.

'No,' I say, 'the guru is not God. He is considered to be an ambassador of God and therefore should be given all respects, just as the ambassador of the Queen receives all respects, but he is not the Queen. Actually,' I say, shocking him, 'the guru is like a postman delivering a letter.'

'It is written in scripture,' he insists, misquoting Bhagavad Gita again.

'No,' I say, 'the quote is "Guru is as good as God" and only because he brings the message of God.'

'No,' he argues.

'Please,' I ask him gently, 'show me the quotation in Bhagavad Gita.'

Finding the place he seems surprised, 'Oh, yes, yes, you are correct,' he admits.

He leaves us then, going deep into the back of the compound and returns with two oranges, icy cold and sweet from the luxury of a buried refrigerator. 'Who is she?' he asks Razzaque in Bengali.

'She is my spiritual master,' he answers.

*   *   *   *

Airport and goodbyes today. The planes hooking into the trackless skies. I hate the leavings, hate the losings. The Dhaka airport's choc-a-bloc with goodbyes, was actually built for it. It's written into the ticket, the taxi, the passports are stamped with it.

I press my face against a bouquet of fresh lilies, *rajuni gunda*, whose thick white flesh cools my flushed cheek. I study the pale green stems parcelled together by a grey rubber band, telling Razzaque, 'I can't give you an answer about the teaching now.' Hedging I say, 'I'll give it serious thought. Let you know what I decide when I return from London.'

Naturally, there is a crush of Bengalis. The men in unaccustomed suits, clumping proudly in shiny shoes, their wives, with babies attached dressed in their finery, wedding saris, Sunday best, a razzle of colour and gold. These warm, sunny people, so open and affectionate, hopeful and happy, their suitcases packed with dreams make my heart ache. I worry about them. They aren't used to the cold and England can be so cold.

'Goodbye,' I say again, unshed tears rising in my eyes. Blinking hard, I look away and notice one of the airport cleaners taking a break, leaning against a wall. The 'C' has somehow come off his uniform leaving 'LEANER' written across his back, making me giggle. 'What a crazy world this is,' I say to Razzaque who looks and begins to laugh. Prabhupada always used to tell us, 'this world is no place for a gentleman.'

*   *   *   *

One who knows and does not teach incurs the judgement of God.

By day I may appear calm, cool, and collected, but under the table sex is rolling its marbles around. At night in my narrow bed, wet heart attacks of lust disturb my dreams. After almost ten years of celibacy, without difficulty, I'm ashamed to find myself victim of a relapse of sexual desire. 'Oh great renouncer of the world,' I laugh at myself, 'You are supposed to be a spiritual master, not a spiritual mistress.'

In the mornings, the window is crowded by an English

sky, juicy with rain. I stagger from my bed shaking with exhaustion, my struggles tattooed on the skin around my eyes, feeling so fragile I fear my feet will splinter on the bare wooden floor boards.

I run to Father Tracey for shelter and advice. After hearing me out, he says, kindly, 'Having desire is not a sin, Rytasha. I believe you are being tested before a great mission which you are about to begin.' Yes, I think. Our tests are tailormade to our weakness. The devil doesn't offer a starving man a naked woman, he offers him bread.

'Jamuna?' I ask, 'Would you think I was crazy to teach.'

'Rytasha,' she answers, 'I would think you were crazy if you didn't teach.'

One! I say to God I will take one, but only one!

Having finally surrendered I find myself at peace. Though it may appear that I am leading, in reality I am following also. Speaking, I am hearing, realizing that the actual spiritual master is always God.

To know and not to do is not really to know. Knowledge at its deepest level is lived. Life itself has become a religious experience. Travelling, working, making plans to build a free clinic, setting up new projects, teaching. We do not leave life undone.

*　*　*　*

Ramsara, morning, the children racing towards school. A little boy who runs after them, stumbling along on gawky legs, sometimes falling down, getting up awkwardly, desperately trying to keep up and all the while calling pathetically after them to wait for him, as they run on ahead of him unheeding, laughing and giggling together. He's such a funny-looking little guy, with a stubble cap of hair, jug ears, a little rodent face which he screws up as he negotiates the steps of the school by leaning down and feeling along the ground with his hands. Suddenly it occurs to me that he must be blind, a poor blind mouse.

I ask the teachers and find out that, though he can hardly see, by listening carefully he's become a good student and by holding the book right up to his eye, his nose touching the page, he has managed to learn to read and write. Like a flower trying to grow through rock and almost succeeding. Even though his future will be the streets and begging, at least he won't see the people who turn away leaving him hungry and lonely.

Hoping for a miracle, I decide to take him to Khulna to the eye clinic where a friend of ours is the doctor in charge.

I get his parents' permission: poor, work-worn, landless people who come out of their tiny bamboo hut with a few *taka* wrapped in a bit of cloth 'for his bus fare'. No, of course not; I thank them, my heart aching at their simple hope.

Razzaque, myself and one of our teachers, who will stay with him, take him with us when we leave, travelling by cart to the main road where we catch the bus. Never having been away from home, his small village and his mother, riding in a bus for the first time but not able to see what is happening around him; the noise, the smells and strange people, the motion of the bumping bus makes him sick to his stomach.

In Khulna city he stumbles and almost falls getting

down the high steps from the bus, his threadbare shirt stained with vomit, his mouth hanging open as he strains to get his bearings. Yet through it all, hope shines out of him so strongly that I feel a pang of fear. Oh Lord, what have I done? What if he can't be cured, I worry.

I'm nervous and sleepless until I hear the doctor's verdict. 'It's juvenile cataracts and, yes, his eyesight can be restored.' The doctor tells us that normally cataracts appear in people aged sixty-five to seventy in the West, but because of malnutrition and the terrible living conditions in Bangladesh, a country where the average life expectancy is thirty-seven, they usually appear much earlier. 'Leave him with me at the clinic for a week,' he says. 'Let me build him up with some vitamins and minerals in preparation for the operation.'

Razzaque and I must go on to another village project but we return after a few days to see how he is getting on. He is the pet of the clinic, the nurses' helper, leading the patients with bandaged eyes carefully down the hallways and feeding them their dinners. He comes out to show us a new shirt his mother has sent him. He is so proud of it that I don't have the heart to tell him he's got it on inside out.

*　*　*　*

While the village dozes I lean my back against the cool grey-green back of a tree hung with plump fruit sugaring in its rosy skin, giving class to Razzaque, watched by a white cow, with blissful almond eyes, who rests peacefully beside me on the warm earth.

'May I listen?' asks Kesto, a quiet young man, leader of the men's group and the son of the house where we are staying. 'Of course, you are most welcome,' I say.

The next day he brings a friend and respectfully requests, 'May he also hear Mataji?'

Day by day the room in the cooler clay house where we now hold class becomes more and more crowded as the men go back and tell others about what they have heard. Soon the people have overflowed on to the porch and the area outside the house.

One day Kesto comes with a request, 'Mataji, will you come and speak to the people?' 'Yes,' I agree.

The day of the meeting Razzaque insists I take rest after a lunch of boiled potatoes and tomatoes. Not realizing how tired I have become from a morning spent working with various women's groups, walking miles to visit their houses, I lie down on the bed made of planks of wood and fall immediately into a deep sleep.

Sleeping I dream I'm in a garden, an abandoned garden, overgrown with weeds and neglect. Gurudeva is there. Seeing him again fills me with a bitter-sweet joy. 'Rytasha,' he says, 'tend my garden.'

I wake with tears streaming down my face and I cry and I cry, the dream slowly fading as I become more and more awake; cast out, the fresh wound slowly closing. 'Tend my garden,' he had said. I don't understand, but there isn't time to think about it now anyway, for we must leave immediately or be late.

Coming across the fields, just before dusk I'm chanting the holy name and, though my mind is fixed on God, my heart trembles, is humbled when I see thousands of people waiting.

Turning within to the smallness of myself I pray at the edge of inspiration. 'By the grace of God, a lame man may cross impassible mountains. By the grace of God, a blind man may see the stars in the night sky. And by the grace of God, a dumb man may recite beautiful poetry. Only by the grace of God.' Fulfilling myself in renouncing myself I preach; into the hours. Speak and answer.

'Mataji, there are so many rules and regulations, it is said in scriptures, a man must keep. How shall I know what to do, what is right and what is wrong action?'

'Believing firmly in God's protection accept all things which are favourable to the devotional service of the Lord and reject all things which are unfavourable.'

'Must I give up everything I own?' a young man asks.

'What do you own?' I ask. 'Everything already belongs to God. We may only have the use of things, while we are here. So it's not a matter of giving up things, but of using them correctly . . . in God's service.'

'What shall I do, that I may see God?' another asks.

'Don't try to see God, but act in such a way that God sees you.'

'Mataji, Mataji, of all the religions, which one is the best religion?'

'That religion is the best, which gives you love of God.'

The haunting sound of a flute calls across the fields. I close my eyes . . . and remember . . . yes, now it will begin. I will leave behind the city of my mind with its smoky illusions and concrete heart. I shall lock my house and close the windows against the rain of tears. I will travel to a secret country to meet my Lord.

There the fields are flat unto eternity and the sky is the colour of desire.